PUBLIC HEALTH IN THE 21ST CENTURY

GENETIC INFORMATION, HEALTH LAWS, WELLNESS PROGRAMS AND EMPLOYMENT

IMPLICATIONS AND INTERACTIONS

PUBLIC HEALTH IN THE 21ST CENTURY

Additional books in this series can be found on Nova's website under the Series tab.

Additional E-books in this series can be found on Nova's website under the E-book tab.

GENETICS – RESEARCH AND ISSUES

Additional books in this series can be found on Nova's website under the Series tab.

Additional E-books in this series can be found on Nova's website under the E-book tab.

PUBLIC HEALTH IN THE 21ST CENTURY

GENETIC INFORMATION, HEALTH LAWS, WELLNESS PROGRAMS AND EMPLOYMENT

IMPLICATIONS AND INTERACTIONS

ANTHONY F. GOSSLING
AND
JIM RICHARDS
EDITORS

Nova Science Publishers, Inc.
New York

For permission to use material from this book please contact us:
Telephone 631-231-7269; Fax 631-231-8175
Web Site: http://www.novapublishers.com

Library of Congress Cataloging-in-Publication Data

ISBN 978-1-61942-176-9

Published by Nova Science Publishers, Inc. † New York

CONTENTS

PREFACE

This book provides a brief overview of GINA, an overview of relevant PPACA and GINA provisions relating to the provision of health insurance through the private market and the implementation of employer wellness programs, and statutory analysis of the potential interactions between the related provision in both laws.

Chapter 1- Upon the enactment of the Patient Protection and Affordable Care Act (PPACA), as amended, certain questions have been raised about how PPACA might affect existing law. One such existing law, the Genetic Information Nondiscrimination Act (GINA), is a civil rights statute and has as its purpose the prohibition of discrimination against individuals on the basis of genetic information. In order to effectuate this prohibition, GINA not only contains certain requirements for health insurance and a general prohibition of employment discrimination provisions, but also has strong privacy protections. On the other hand, PPACA is comprehensive health care legislation that is intended to, among other things, enhance consumer protections in the private health insurance market. Both GINA and PPACA contain provisions affecting certain elements of health insurance, as well as employment-based wellness programs. PPACA, the more recent statute, does not specifically amend GINA and also does not reference GINA's requirements. The two laws serve different but complementary purposes, and there is no explicit conflict or contradiction in their terms. Still, the interaction of these two acts may be analyzed.

Chapter 2- Health reform is a major issue on the domestic policy agenda of the Congress. Congress has been considering a number of policy proposals to reform the health delivery system that aim to improve health care quality, reduce health care costs, and expand access to care. A range of proposals have targeted reform of the delivery system through an increased focus on prevention and wellness in an effort to encourage individuals to adopt healthier lifestyles. One prominent policy lever being considered in some health delivery reform proposals is employer wellness programs. Employer wellness programs often focus on improving wellness overall, but may target a specific disease (e.g., diabetes) or behavior (e.g., smoking), may include the provision of a range of health or other services, and are offered by employers to employees through the workplace or other setting.

Chapter 3- Health care costs have risen dramatically in recent years, and employers providing health insurance, as well as other insurance providers, have struggled to find ways to contain costs. This has led to the introduction of incentives to promote healthy behaviors, often referred to as wellness programs. These programs take a myriad of forms from providing a gym at the workplace to subsidizing the co-pays of certain medications and linking health care benefits or discounts to certain healthy lifestyles. In Arkansas, for example, state employees who exercise more frequently or eat healthier foods can earn up to three extra days off from work each year. These healthy lifestyle programs can include requirements for no tobacco use as well as requirements for certain cholesterol, blood pressure, or body mass index (BMI) measurements. For example, Scotts Miracle-Gro, a lawn care company, announced a policy that any smoking by employees, whether on or off the job, would result in termination of employment.

Chapter 4- The Genetic Information Nondiscrimination Act of 2008 (GINA) prohibits discrimination based on genetic information by health insurers and employers. GINA is divided into two main parts: Title I, which prohibits discrimination based on genetic information by health insurers; and Title II, which prohibits discrimination in employment based on genetic information. Title II of GINA prohibits discrimination in employment because of genetic information and, with certain exceptions, prohibits an employer from requesting, requiring, or purchasing genetic information. The law prohibits the use of genetic information in employment decisions—including hiring, firing, job assignments, and promotions—by employers, unions, employment agencies, and labor management training programs and mandates confidential treatment of any genetic information that is obtained.

Chapter 5- The Genetic Information Nondiscrimination Act of 2008 (GINA) prohibits discrimination based on genetic information by health insurers and employers. GINA is divided into two main parts: Title I, which prohibits discrimination based on genetic information by health insurers; and Title II, which prohibits discrimination in employment based on genetic information. Title II of GINA prohibits discrimination in employment because of genetic information and, with certain exceptions, prohibits an employer from requesting, requiring, or purchasing genetic information. The law prohibits the use of genetic information in employment decisions—including hiring, firing, job assignments, and promotions—by employers, unions, employment agencies, and labor management training programs and mandates confidential treatment of any genetic information that is obtained.

Chapter 6- On May 21, 2008, the Genetic Information Nondiscrimination Act of 2008 (GINA), referred to by its sponsors as the first civil rights act of the 21st century, was enacted. GINA, P.L. 110-233, prohibits discrimination based on genetic information by health insurers and employers. The sequencing of the human genome and subsequent advances raise hope for genetic therapies to cure disease, but this scientific accomplishment is not without potential problems. An employer or health insurer could decide to take adverse action based on a genetic predisposition to disease, and situations have arisen where discriminatory action based on genetic information did occur. In addition, there is evidence that the fear of genetic discrimination has an adverse effect on those seeking genetic testing, as well as on participation in genetic research. GINA was enacted to remedy this situation.

In: Genetic Information, Health Laws ... ISBN: 978-1-61942-176-9
Editors: Gossling and Richards

Chapter 1

The Genetic Information Nondiscrimination Act of 2008 and the Patient Protection and Affordable Care Act of 2010: Overview and Legal Analysis of Potential Interactions

Amanda K. Sarata, Nancy Lee Jones and Jennifer Staman

Summary

Upon the enactment of the Patient Protection and Affordable Care Act (PPACA), as amended, certain questions have been raised about how PPACA might affect existing law. One such existing law, the Genetic Information Nondiscrimination Act (GINA), is a civil rights statute and has as its purpose the prohibition of discrimination against individuals on the basis of genetic information. In order to effectuate this prohibition, GINA not only contains certain requirements for health insurance and a general prohibition of employment discrimination provisions, but also has strong privacy protections. On the other hand, PPACA is comprehensive health care legislation that is intended to, among other things, enhance consumer protections in the private health insurance market. Both GINA and PPACA contain provisions affecting certain elements of health insurance, as well as employment-based wellness programs. PPACA, the more recent statute, does not specifically amend GINA and also does not reference GINA's requirements. The two laws serve different but complementary purposes, and there is no explicit conflict or contradiction in their terms. Still, the interaction of these two acts may be analyzed.

This report provides a brief overview of GINA, an overview of relevant PPACA and GINA provisions relating to the provision of health insurance through the private market and the implementation of employer wellness programs, and statutory analysis of the potential interactions between the related provisions in both laws.

BACKGROUND

With the passage of health reform law, interest has turned to determining not only how the new law may be interpreted and implemented, but also how it may interact with existing law. The Patient Protection and Affordable Care Act of 2010 (PPACA, P.L. 111-148, as modified by the Health Care and Education Reconciliation Act, P.L. 111-152), among other things, created a number of significant reforms to the private health insurance market. These reforms include changes that will limit the ability of a group health plan or health insurance issuer to set premiums or determine eligibility for coverage based on criteria such as health status. Title I of the Genetic Information Nondiscrimination Act of 2008 (GINA, P.L. 110-233) also contains requirements affecting health insurance premiums and coverage eligibility, and thus questions may be raised about the potential for interaction between these two Acts.

In addition, PPACA includes provisions relating to the implementation of employer wellness programs. Title II of GINA prohibits discrimination in employment based on genetic information and generally prohibits the collection of genetic information. However, there is a specific exception for wellness programs with attendant privacy protections. This raises questions about the potential for interaction between these two sets of provisions, specifically with respect to requirements around the release of genetic information and incentives for participation in such a program.

This report provides a brief overview of GINA, an overview of relevant PPACA and GINA provisions relating to the provision of health insurance through the private market, an overview of relevant PPACA and GINA provisions relating to the implementation of employer wellness programs, and statutory analysis of the potential interactions between the related provisions in both laws.[1]

GINA Overview

On May 21, 2008, the Genetic Information Nondiscrimination Act of 2008 (GINA), referred to by its sponsors as the first civil rights act of the 21st century, was enacted. GINA prohibits discrimination by health insurers and employers based on genetic information. Genetic information is considered sensitive for a number of reasons, including that it may be predictive or indicate a predisposition to disease, and that it can affect not only an individual but also family members.[2]

GINA is divided into two main parts: Title I, which prohibits discrimination in health insurance based on genetic information, and Title II, which prohibits discrimination in employment based on genetic information. Title I of GINA amends the Employee Retirement Income Security Act of 1974 (ERISA), the Public Health Services Act (PHSA), and the Internal Revenue Code (IRC),[3] as well as the Social Security Act (SSA), to prohibit group health plans[4] and health insurance issuers[5] providing group and individual health coverage from engaging in genetic discrimination and to strengthen and clarify existing HIPAA nondiscrimination and portability provisions with respect to genetic information and genetic testing.[6] The complexity of the health care financing system required this multifaceted approach in order to ensure protection for all individuals, regardless of their coverage arrangements. [7] On October 7, 2009, the Departments of Labor, Health and Human Services, and Treasury issued interim final regulations implementing the majority of provisions in Title I of GINA. These regulations became effective as of December 7, 2009, and specifically for plan years beginning on or after December 7, 2009, for group health plans and health insurance issuers.[8] In addition, also on October 7, 2009, the Department of Health and Human Services (Office for Civil Rights) issued a proposed rule which would implement §105 of GINA.[9]

Title II of GINA prohibits discrimination in employment based on genetic information and, with certain exceptions, prohibits an employer from requesting, requiring, or purchasing genetic information. The law prohibits the use of genetic information in employment decisions— including hiring, firing, job assignments, and promotions—by employers, unions, employment agencies, and labor management training programs. On November 9, 2010, the Equal Employment Opportunity Commission (EEOC) issued final regulations for Title II that take effect on January 10, 2010. These regulations generally closely track the statutory language.[10]

GINA TITLE I AND PPACA

Introduction

GINA prohibits the use of genetic information in determining premiums for individuals or groups or for serving as the basis for conditioning health coverage. PPACA, on the other hand, specifically defines the factors on which insurers may predicate issuance of coverage or determination of premiums. Thus, questions may be raised as to how the two statutes might interact with one another in the specific area of private health insurance market reforms. This section provides an overview of relevant GINA and PPACA provisions concerning coverage eligibility and premium determination to provide context for a statutory analysis outlining the potential interactions between the relevant provisions.

GINA

Broadly, GINA prohibits group health plans and health insurance issuers from engaging in three practices: (1) using genetic information about an individual to adjust a group plan's premiums, or, in the case of individual plans, to deny coverage, adjust premiums, or impose a preexisting condition exclusion;[11] (2) requesting, requiring, or purchasing genetic information for underwriting purposes or prior to enrollment; and (3) requiring or requesting genetic testing. Each of these prohibitions is discussed below in more detail.

Premium Determination

GINA prohibits health plans, group and individual health insurance issuers, and issuers of Medicare supplemental policies from adjusting a group or individual's premium or contribution amount based on genetic information about an individual in the group, an individual seeking individual coverage, or an individual's family members.[12]

Collection and Use of Genetic Information Restricted

GINA prohibits health plans, group and individual health insurers and issuers, and issuers of Medicare supplemental policies from requesting, requiring, or purchasing genetic information for the purposes of underwriting or prior to an individual's enrollment or in connection with enrollment.[13] "Incidental collection" of genetic information—genetic information obtained incidentally to the requesting, requiring, or purchasing of other information concerning any individual—would not be considered a violation of the prohibition on collecting genetic information prior to enrollment if it is not done for underwriting purposes. "Underwriting purposes," as defined by GINA, includes (1) rules for, or determination of, eligibility for benefits; (2) the computation of premium or contribution amounts; (3) the application of any preexisting condition exclusion; and (4) other activities related to the creation, renewal, or replacement of a contract of health insurance or health benefits.[14]

GINA also prohibits individual insurers from conditioning eligibility or continuing eligibility on genetic information, and prohibits individual insurers from treating genetic information as a preexisting condition. Issuers of supplemental Medicare policies may not deny or condition the issuance of a policy based on genetic information (and may not impose a preexisting condition exclusion based on genetic information).[15]

Genetic Testing Requirements Prohibited

GINA prohibits health plans, group and individual health insurance issuers, and issuers of Medicare supplemental policies from requesting or requiring that individuals or their family members undergo a genetic test.[16] This prohibition does not limit the authority of a health care professional to request that an individual undergo genetic testing as part of his or her course of health care. The Act provides for a research exception to this provision, by allowing a group or individual insurance issuer to request, but not require, an individual to undergo genetic testing if specific conditions are met.[17]

PPACA

As noted above, PPACA creates new federal standards applicable to private health insurance coverage. While some of the new federal standards begin to take effect this year, others take effect for plan years beginning on or after January 1, 2014. Among these later reforms, PPACA establishes new rating requirements that allow insurers to vary premiums based only on certain key characteristics.[18] These characteristics are self or family enrollment in a plan or coverage; rating area (as established by a state and reviewed by the Secretary); age (by no more than a 3:1 ratio across age rating bands established by the Secretary, in consultation with the National Association of Insurance Commissioners [NAIC]); and tobacco use (by no more than a 1.5:1 ratio). Thus, health insurance issuers subject to this provision are precluded from charging premiums based on health factors and other additional criteria (e.g., the sex of the covered individual). Further, PPACA prohibits group health plans and health insurance issuers in the individual and group markets from excluding coverage for preexisting health conditions. [19] While group health plans and health insurance issuers may not impose any preexisting condition exclusion on enrollees who are under 19 years of age for plan years beginning on or after six months after enactment (i.e., September 23, 2010), this prohibition becomes applicable to other enrollees in 2014.

In addition, PPACA requires individual and group health insurance issuers to offer coverage on a guaranteed issue and guaranteed renewal basis.[20] Under the Act, health insurance issuers offering health insurance coverage in the individual or group market in a state must accept every employer and individual in the state that applies for such coverage, subject to certain conditions. Further, PPACA provides that health insurance issuers offering coverage in the individual or group market must renew or continue in force such coverage at the option of the plan sponsor or the individual, subject to exceptions such as nonpayment of premiums, or an act or practice of fraud.[21] Thus, based on these provisions, a health insurance issuer would be precluded from denying coverage, or denying a renewal of coverage, based on factors such as the individual's health.

Analysis of Title I of GINA and PPACA

In examining provisions of GINA in relation to comparable provisions in Title I of PPACA pertaining to health insurance, there appears to be some overlap in the reach of these Acts. For example, under GINA, a group health plan and a health insurance issuer may not adjust premium or contribution amounts on the basis of genetic information.[22] Alternatively, under section 2701 of the PHSA, as created by PPACA, certain health insurance issuers may only vary premiums based on certain specified factors (i.e., tobacco use, age, geographic area, and self-only or family enrollment). In evaluating the interaction of these two statutes, one may argue that it is possible to read these statutes together as establishing non-conflicting limitations on insurance premiums. While PPACA creates criteria for premium rates, GINA prohibits premium adjustments based on genetic information. Further, it seems that a health insurance issuer can simultaneously comply with the requirements of PPACA and GINA. While a violation of this provision of GINA may also be a violation of section 2701 of the PHSA, there does not appear to be a barrier to offering penalties for the same conduct under these two statutes. Though one may argue that section 2701 of the PHSA renders GINA, at least in part, ineffective and therefore amends or repeals GINA by implication, given that amendments by implication are disfavored, and without a demonstrated clear intention to override its provisions,[23] a court may be more likely to dismiss this argument.

Further, it should be noted that these provisions of PPACA and GINA are not identical in scope. For example, the limitations on premium amounts as added by PPACA apply only to health insurance issuers in the individual and small group markets, and do not apply (as GINA does), for example, to self-insured group health plans or insurers in the large group market. Further, this section of PPACA applies only to premium rates, whereas GINA applies to premiums as well as contribution amounts.[24] The provisions of GINA seem likely to remain intact, because the reach of GINA is beyond that of PPACA and, where there is not a direct conflict, courts are reluctant to amend or repeal a statute by implication.

As discussed above, GINA also prohibits group health plans and health insurance issuers from requesting, requiring, or purchasing genetic information for the purposes of underwriting or prior to an individual's enrollment or in connection with enrollment. As mentioned above, underwriting purposes include, among other things, rules or determination of eligibility for benefits, the application of any preexisting condition exclusion, and other activities related to the creation, renewal, or replacement of a contract of health insurance or health benefits. PPACA, however, curtails application of these underwriting practices and contains requirements related to insurance enrollment. For example, under PPACA, a group health plan and a health insurance issuer will no longer be able to impose a preexisting condition exclusion.[25] In addition, as discussed above, health insurance issuers must accept every individual and employer that applies for coverage and renew or continue such coverage at the option of the plan sponsor or individual. Thus, it seems that the provisions of PPACA may obviate some of the requirements of GINA. If a health insurance issuer generally cannot use certain underwriting practices or limit enrollment to certain individuals, they may not be inclined to obtain genetic information for these purposes. However, this is not to say that GINA is therefore repealed by PPACA. It is likely that a court may read these statutes in concert with each other: while PPACA removes certain limitations to obtaining health insurance, GINA prohibits obtaining genetic information as part of certain insurance practices. Further, it should also be noted that these provisions of GINA and PPACA are also not identical in scope. For example, the guaranteed availability and renewability requirements of PPACA apply only to health insurance issuers and, accordingly, the effects of this provision of GINA on self-insured group health plans may not be affected by PPACA.[26]

Finally, in terms of the prohibition on group health plans and health insurers from requiring an individual or family member to undergo a genetic test, there does not seem to be a comparable provision in PPACA. Given no express language in PPACA that alters this provision, and because PPACA does not seem to have a requirement that interacts with this provision, it appears that this requirement is also not affected by PPACA.

GINA Title II and PPACA

Introduction

GINA and PPACA both include provisions that relate specifically to employer wellness programs, although neither statute specifically requires the use of wellness programs. In GINA, the relevant provisions are limited to the conditions under which an employer might lawfully collect genetic information pursuant to an employer wellness program. PPACA's provisions are broader, encourage the use of wellness programs, and include specifics about these programs, including the extent of financial incentives that an employer may use to encourage participation in wellness programs. This raises questions about the potential interaction between these two statutes with respect to employer wellness programs. This section provides an overview of relevant employer wellness program provisions in GINA and PPACA to provide context for a statutory analysis of the potential interactions between these provisions.

Employer Wellness Programs

Health care costs have risen dramatically in recent years,[27] and employers providing health insurance, as well as other insurance providers, have struggled to find ways to contain costs. This has led to the introduction of incentives to promote healthy behaviors, often referred to as wellness programs. These programs take a myriad of forms, from providing a gym at the workplace to subsidizing the co-pays of certain medications and linking health care benefits or discounts to certain healthy lifestyles. In Arkansas, for example, state employees who exercise more frequently or eat healthier foods can earn up to three extra days off from work each year.[28] These healthy lifestyle programs can include requirements for no tobacco use, as well as requirements for certain cholesterol, blood pressure, and body mass index (BMI) measurements.[29]

GINA

Most, if not all, employer wellness programs collect medical information from participants. Programs may request or require participating employees to answer questions about family history of certain diseases, conditions, or disorders. This information falls under the definition of genetic information under GINA, and therefore its acquisition and use by employers is strictly regulated and is protected differently than is employer acquisition of other medical information.[30]

GINA broadly prohibits both the acquisition of genetic information, as well as the use of genetic information by employers in employment decisions; however, it does provide for several exceptions to the prohibition on employer acquisition of this information. Specifically, Title II of GINA allows employers, employment agencies, labor organizations, and training programs to acquire genetic information pursuant to the offering of health or genetic services, including services offered as part of a wellness program.[31] The statute states, in pertinent part, "[i]t shall be an unlawful employment practice for an employer to request, require, or purchase genetic information with respect to an employee or a family member of the employee except – ... (2) where health or genetic services are offered by the employer, including such services offered as part of a wellness program."[32] The exception provided for by this provision is materially identical for employment agencies, labor organizations, and training programs.[33]

However, employers may collect genetic information as part of a wellness program, pursuant to this exception, *only* if they meet three requirements:

- the employee must provide prior, knowing, voluntary, and written authorization;
- only the employee and the licensed health care professional or board-certified genetic counselor involved in providing such services receive individually identifiable information concerning the results of such services; and
- any individually identifiable genetic information provided in connection with the health or genetic services provided under this exception is only available for the purposes of such services and shall not be disclosed to the employer except in aggregate terms that do not disclose the identity of specific employees.[34]

The EEOC final regulations reiterate the exception for wellness programs and its requirements.[35] In the proposed regulations, EEOC emphasized that such programs must be voluntary, and asked for comments concerning the appropriate level of inducement offered for participation in a wellness program. In the final regulations, the EEOC concluded that inducements may be offered to encourage individuals to participate in wellness programs, but inducements may not be offered to provide genetic information. The EEOC provides the following example in the regulations as a situation that does not violate GINA:

> A covered entity offers $150 to employees who complete a health risk assessment with 100 questions, the last 20 of them concerning family medical history and other genetic information. The instructions for completing the health risk assessment make clear that the inducement will be provided to all employees who respond to the first 80 questions, whether or not the remaining 20 questions concerning family medical history and other genetic information are answered.[36]

However, if the health risk assessment does not make clear which questions must be answered, it would violate GINA.[37]

Similarly, the regulations state that financial inducements may be offered to encourage participation in wellness programs for individuals who have voluntarily provided genetic information. In order to comply with GINA, these programs must also be offered to individuals with health conditions or life style choices that put them at an increased risk of developing a condition. For example, it would not violate GINA to offer $150 for participation in a weight loss program to employees who voluntarily disclose a family history of diabetes, heart disease, or high blood pressure, and to employees who have a current diagnosis of one of these conditions.[38]

Importantly, regardless of how an employer may acquire genetic information (either inadvertently or through these exceptions), the employer is still absolutely prohibited from using the information to discriminate in employment decisions, such as hiring, firing, and promotion.

PPACA

PPACA contains several provisions specifically relating to wellness programs.[39] Of most significance in the context of a discussion of GINA are

- PPACA § 1001, which creates a new §27 17 in the Public Health Services Act (PHSA) concerning reporting requirements for group health plans;
- PPACA § 1201, which creates a new §2705 in the PHSA prohibiting discrimination on the basis of health status;
- PPACA §4303, amended by §10404 of P.L. 111-152, creates sections in the PHSA, including section 399MM, which provides for Centers for Disease Control (CDC) technical assistance for employer-based wellness programs; and
- PPACA § 10408, concerning workplace wellness grants.[40]

The new §2705 in the PHSA (PPACA § 1201) prohibits discrimination by group health plans and health insurance issuers on the basis of health status and specifically includes genetic information as a health status related factor. Effective for plan years beginning on or after January 1, 2014, this section generally codifies HIPAA wellness program regulations.[41] Wellness programs that do not require the satisfaction of a standard relating to a health factor and are made available to all similarly situated individuals are not considered discriminatory. If, however, a wellness program conditions receiving a reward (such as a premium rebate) on meeting a health factor-related standard (such as a blood pressure measurement), there are specific requirements, including a cap on the amount of the reward. The reward in these situations must be capped at 30% of the cost of the employee-only coverage under the plan.

Under pre-PPACA HIPAA regulations, the cap was set at 20%. In addition, under PPACA the Secretaries of HHS, Labor, and Treasury have the discretion to increase this reward to up to 50%.[42] Wellness programs that provide a reward must also

- be reasonably designed to promote health or prevent disease and not be a subterfuge for discriminating based on a health status factor;
- provide eligible individuals the opportunity to qualify for the reward at least once a year;
- be available to all similarly situated individuals; and
- disclose in all plan materials the availability of a reasonable alternative standard or the possibility of a waiver.

The requirement that the program be available to similarly situated individuals is further elaborated on in PPACA. The law states that this requirement is not met unless the wellness program allows for "a reasonable alternative standard (or waiver of the otherwise applicable standard) for obtaining the reward for any individual for whom, for that period, it is unreasonably difficult due to a medical condition to satisfy the otherwise applicable standard" or for whom is it is medically inadvisable to attempt to satisfy the otherwise applicable standard. PPACA allows the plan or issuer, "if reasonable under the circumstances," to seek verification "such as a statement from an individual's physician, that a health status factor makes it unreasonably difficult or medically inadvisable for the individual to satisfy or attempt to satisfy the otherwise applicable standard."

The other three PPACA sections mentioned above, PPACA § § 1001, 4303, and 10408, all encourage the provision of wellness programs.

Analysis of Title II of GINA and PPACA

Both Title II of GINA and PPACA include provisions relating to wellness programs, although the statutes have a different focus. PPACA addresses wellness programs as a means to increase the health of employees and reduce medical costs; Title II of GINA prohibits employment discrimination, generally prohibiting employers from collecting genetic information, and contains broad privacy protections. GINA permits the collection of genetic information for the purpose of wellness programs and contains detailed requirements including, for example, written authorization for the collection of this data. PPACA does not contain similar privacy protections and does not address its relationship with GINA; however, the two statutes do not directly contradict one another. Thus, it could be argued that the disfavored statutory construction approach of repeal by implication would not be appropriate; the two statutes can be read in a complementary manner. [43]

Another rule of statutory construction states that where there is a conflict between the statutes, the most recent statute generally takes precedence.[44] However, it would appear that the provisions of PPACA and GINA are complementary, not contradictory. Like the previous analysis, PPACA and Title II of GINA could be read together in such a way as to give effect to both. Although PPACA does not contain the specific detailed privacy provisions regarding wellness programs contained in GINA, it could be argued that GINA's provisions supplement the PPACA nondiscrimination requirements. This argument is further supported by the fact that the nondiscrimination requirements were in the pre-PPACA version of HIPAA and the HIPAA regulations contained similar, but not identical, requirements relating to wellness programs. It could even be contended that reading the provisions together would advance the PPACA goal of prohibiting discrimination against individuals based on health status, because privacy protections regarding genetic information would decrease the likelihood of discrimination. Thus, it would appear likely that a court would interpret the wellness provisions of PPACA and Title II of GINA as complementary.

CONCLUSION

As noted above, both GINA and PPACA contain provisions affecting certain elements of health insurance, as well as wellness programs. GINA is a civil rights statute and has as its purpose the prohibition of discrimination against individuals on the basis of genetic information. In order to effectuate this prohibition, GINA not only contains certain requirements for health insurance and a general prohibition of employment discrimination provisions, but also has strong privacy protections. On the other hand, PPACA is comprehensive health care legislation that is intended to, among other things, enhance consumer protections in the private health insurance market and expand health coverage. PPACA, the more recent statute, does not specifically amend GINA and also does not reference GINA's requirements.[45]

Generally, when interpreting the interactions of two statutes that address similar situations or subject matter, courts will try to read the statutes in such a way as to give effect to the language of both. Further, when Congress enacts legislation to amend an existing statute, courts may attempt to read new provisions together with those that were left unchanged and to interpret the provisions so they do not conflict. A leading treatise on statutory construction also notes that repeal of a prior law by implication is disfavored,[46] and observes that "[t]he point of the rules of interpretation is to give harmonious effect to all acts on a subject where reasonably possible."[47] However, where a new statute is a comprehensive revision of a subject area there is "a strong implication of a legislative intent to repeal former statutory law."[48] While PPACA has been described as a comprehensive revision of federal law regarding health care, the Act evidences no intent to be the sole regulation of the health care system. Therefore, courts would be more likely to examine the issue through the specific requirements of the statutes of PPACA and GINA and attempt to reconcile these statutes. This more nuanced approach would appear to better reflect and give full effect to the actual language of GINA and PPACA. Ultimately, the precise landscape of these requirements may await final regulations from these agencies and, perhaps, judicial decisions.

End Notes

[1] PPACA includes provisions for the grandfathering of health insurance plans in existence on the date of enactment of the Act (i.e., March 23, 2010). Grandfathered plans are exempt from the majority of new insurance reforms created by PPACA. It should be noted that some of the issues addressed in this report may not apply to grandfathered plans. For more information on grandfathered plans, see CRS Report R41 166, *Grandfathered Health Plans Under the Patient Protection and Affordable Care Act (PPACA)*, by Bernadette Fernandez.

[2] For more information about GINA, see CRS Report RL34584, *The Genetic Information Nondiscrimination Act of 2008 (GINA)*, by Nancy Lee Jones and Amanda K. Sarata.

[3] In general, Title XVII of the PHSA, along with parallel provisions in Part 7 of ERISA and Subchapter B of chapter 100 of the IRC, govern the nature and content of health insurance coverage provided primarily in the private sector. Prior to PPACA, many of the provisions dealing with the regulation of private health insurance in these three laws were added by the Health Insurance Portability and Accountability Act (HIPAA), which was designed to improve health care access, portability, and renewability. P.L. 104-191, 110 Stat. 1936 (1996). PPACA also amends these three laws to create new requirements for private health coverage.

[4] "Group health plans" may be defined as employee benefit plans (i.e., plans established by an employer or an employer organization) that provide medical care to employees or their dependents directly or through insurance, reimbursement, or otherwise. *See, e.g.*, 42 U.S.C. § 300gg-91(a)(1). A group health plan may include a self-insured plan, which is a plan that is provided by the organization seeking health coverage for its members. Such organizations pay for health benefits directly, as the organization itself bears the risk for covering medical expenses (as opposed to an insurer).

[5] A "health insurance issuer" is an insurance company, insurance service, or insurance organization that is licensed to engage in the business of insurance in a state and that is subject to state law that regulates insurance. 42 U.S.C. § 300gg-91(b)(2).

[6] HIPAA established certain nondiscrimination requirements that are intended to prevent group health plans and health insurance issuers from discriminating against individual participants or beneficiaries based on a "health status-related factor." In particular, HIPAA amended the PHSA, ERISA, and the IRC to prohibit group health plans and health insurance issuers from basing coverage eligibility rules on these health status factors, which include health status (physical or mental), claims experience, receipt of health care, medical history, evidence of insurability, or disability, and genetic information. *See, e.g.,* 29 U.S.C. § 1182. In addition, group health plans and health insurance issuers may not require that an individual pay a higher premium or contribution than another "similarly situated" participant based on these factors. PPACA retains these requirements and extends them to health insurance issuers in the individual market.

[7] In general, the PHSA, ERISA, and the IRC govern different types of health plans and health insurance coverage. For example, the PHSA covers some self-insured group health plans (non-federal governmental plans), as well as health insurance issuers providing group health coverage and coverage in the individual market. See 42 U.S.C. § 300gg-21. ERISA covers group health plans (including private-sector self-insured plans) and health insurance issuers providing group health coverage, and it does not cover governmental plans, church plans, or insurance in the individual market. *See* 29 U.S.C. § 1003. The IRC covers group health plans, including church plans, but does not cover health insurers.

[8] 74 Fed. Reg. 51633 (October 7, 2009).

[9] 74 Fed. Reg. 51698 (October 7, 2009).

[10] 75 Fed. Reg. 68912 (November 9, 2010). For a general discussion of the regulations see CRS Report R41527, *The Genetic Information Nondiscrimination Act (GINA): Final Employment Regulations*, by Nancy Lee Jones.

[11] For purposes of the GINA and PPACA requirements, a "preexisting condition exclusion" means a limitation or exclusion of benefits relating to a condition that was present before the date of enrollment for health coverage, whether or not any medical advice, diagnosis, care, or treatment was recommended or received before such date. 42 U.S.C. § 300gg-3(b)(1)(A). Excluding coverage for preexisting conditions refers to the case in which an applicant for coverage is offered a health insurance policy but that policy does not provide benefits for certain medical conditions.

[12] *See, e.g.,* P.L. 110-233, § 101(a). 29 U.S.C. § 1182(b)(3).

[13] *See, e.g.,* P.L. 110-233, § 101(b). 29 U.S.C. § 1182(d).

[14] *See, e.g.,* P.L. 110-233, § 101(d). 29 U.S.C. § 1191b.

[15] P.L. 110-233, § 104(a). 42 U.S.C. 1395ss(s)(2).

[16] See, e.g., P.L. 110-233, § 101(b). 29 U.S.C. § 1182(c)(1).

[17] See, e.g., P.L. 110-233, § 101(b). 29 U.S.C. § 1182(c)(4).

[18] P.L. 111-148, § 1201 (section 2701 of the PHSA).

[19] P.L. 111-148, § 1201 (section 2704 of the PHSA).

[20] P.L. 111-148, § 1201 (section 2702 of the PHSA).

[21] P.L. 111-148, § 1201 (section 2704 of the PHSA).

[22] *See, e.g.,* P.L. 110-233. Section 202(b); 29 U.S.C. § 1 182(b)(3).

[23] *See e.g.,* United States v. Borden Co., 308 U.S. 188, 198 (1939), as cited in Watt v. Alaska, 451 U.S. 259, 267 (1981).

[24] GINA and its accompanying regulations do not define contribution amounts, but it is possible that contribution amounts encompass certain cost-sharing elements of health insurance coverage, including co-payments and deductibles.

[25] P.L. 111-148, § 1201 (section 2704 of the PHSA).

[26] It should also be noted that the provisions of PPACA discussed in this section do not apply to Medicare supplemental benefits. 42 U.S.C. § 300gg-91(c)(4). Thus, these requirements of GINA are likely unaffected by PPACA.

[27] For a discussion of the health costs of chronic diseases, see http://www.cdc.gov/NCCdphp/overview.htm.

[28] National Conference of State Legislatures, *State Employee Health Benefits* (Updated February 28, 2010).

[29] For a discussion of these types of wellness programs, see Lucinda Jesson, "Weighing the Wellness Programs: The Legal Implications of Imposing Personal Responsibility Obligations," 15 Va. J. Soc. Policy and Law 217 (2008).

[30] Title II of GINA defines genetic information as "with respect to any individual, information about such individual's genetic tests, the genetic tests of family members of such individual, and the manifestation of a disease or disorder in family members of such individual." P.L. 110-233, Section 201(4)(A); 42 U.S.C. §2000ff(4).

[31] P.L. 110-233. Section 202(b)(2), Section 203(b)(2), Section 204(b)(2), and Section 205(b)(2); 42 U.S.C. §§2000ff1(b)(2), 2000ff-2(b)(2), 2000ff-3(b)(2), and 2000ff-4(b)(2).

[32] P.L. 110-233. Section 202(b); 42 U.S.C. §2000ff-1(b).

[33] P.L. 110-233. Section 203(b)(2), Section 204(b)(2), and Section 205(b)(2); 42 U.S.C. §§2000ff-2(b)(2), 2000ff3(b)(2), and 2000ff-4(b)(2).

[34] P.L. 110-233. Section 202(b)(2)(B),(C), and (D); 42 U.S.C. §2000ff-1(b)(2)(B),(C), and (D).

[35] 29 C.F.R. §1635.8(b)(2), 75 FED. REG. 68935 (November 9, 2010).

[36] 29 C.F.R. §1635.8(b)(2)(ii)(A), 75 FED. REG. 68935 (November 9, 2010).

[37] 29 C.F.R. §1635.8(b)(2)(ii)(B), 75 FED. REG. 68935 (November 9, 2010).

[38] 29 C.F.R. §1635.8(b)(2)(iii), 75 FED. REG. 68935 (November 9, 2010).

[39] For a more detailed discussion of these provisions, see CRS Report R40943, *Public Health, Workforce, Quality, and Related Provisions in the Patient Protection and Affordable Care Act (P.L. 111-148)*, coordinated by C. Stephen Redhead and Erin D. Williams, pp. 29-44.

[40] For a discussion of all the PPACA provisions relating to prevention and wellness, see CRS Report R40943, *Public Health, Workforce, Quality, and Related Provisions in the Patient Protection and Affordable Care Act (P.L. 111-148)*, coordinated by C. Stephen Redhead and Erin D. Williams, pp. 29-44.

[41] See 29 C.F.R. § 2590.702(b)(1)(ii); 45 C.F.R. 146.121(b)(1)(ii); 26 C.F.R. § 54.9802-1(b)(1)(ii).

[42] The increase in the amount of the reward available has been lauded by some as encouraging behavioral change that will lead to improved health and lower costs. See Michael O'Donnell, "The Science of Health Promotion," 24 AMERICAN JOURNAL OF HEALTH PROMOTION iv (March/April 2010). However, others have argued that tying premium discounts to achieving certain health standards shifts costs to less healthy individuals who tend to be those with lower incomes. See Roni Caryn Rabin, "Could Health Overall Incentives Hurt Some?" THE NEW YORK TIMES (April 12, 2010); http://www.nytimes.com/2010/04/13/health/13land.html.

[43] *See* IA SUTHERLAND, STATUTES AND STATUTORY CONSTRUCTION § 22:34 (Norman J. Singer ed., 7th ed. 2009 rev.).

[44] "If two acts of a legislature are applicable to the same subject, their provisions are to be reconciled if this can be done by fair and reasonable intendment, if however, they are repugnant to one another, the last one enacted shall prevail." Sutherland at § 23:18, footnote 8.

[45] It should be noted that GINA is already in effect, but several of the relevant PPACA provisions discussed in this report do not take effect until 2014. Thus, any potential interactions between the two acts would not occur until various provisions of PPACA become effective.

[46] Sutherland at § 23:11. *See also,* Morton v. Mancari, 417 U.S. 535, 549-551 (1974); U.S. v. Joya-Martinez, 947 F.2d 1141 (4th Cir. 1991)("An implied amendment or partial repeal of a statute will not be recognized by the courts, unless it clearly appears the legislature so

intended."). This presumption against implied amendment or repeal can be overridden, but it takes strong evidence of a legislative intent to do so. *Id.*

[47] Sutherland at § 23.11. As the Supreme Court has noted, "[i]t is a fundamental canon of statutory construction that the words of a statute must be read in their context and with a view to their place in the overall statutory scheme.... A court must therefore interpret the statute 'as a symmetrical and coherent regulatory scheme,' and 'fit, if possible, all parts into an harmonious whole.'" FDA v. Brown & Williamson Tobacco Corp., 529 U.S. 120, 133 (2000).

[48] Sutherland at § 23:13.

In: Genetic Information, Health Laws ... ISBN: 978-1-61942-176-9
Editors: Gossling and Richards

Chapter 2

EMPLOYER WELLNESS PROGRAMS: HEALTH REFORM AND THE GENETIC INFORMATION NONDISCRIMINATION ACT*

Amanda K. Sarata

SUMMARY

Health reform is a major issue on the domestic policy agenda of the Congress. Congress has been considering a number of policy proposals to reform the health delivery system that aim to improve health care quality, reduce health care costs, and expand access to care. A range of proposals have targeted reform of the delivery system through an increased focus on prevention and wellness in an effort to encourage individuals to adopt healthier lifestyles. One prominent policy lever being considered in some health delivery reform proposals is employer wellness programs. Employer wellness programs often focus on improving wellness overall, but may target a specific disease (e.g., diabetes) or behavior (e.g., smoking), may include the provision of a range of health or other services, and are offered by employers to employees through the workplace or other setting.

* This is an edited, reformatted and augmented version of a Congressional Research Service publication, CRS Report for Congress R40791, from www.crs.gov, dated February 16, 2010.

Most if not all employer wellness programs collect medical information from participants. Programs may request or require participating employees to answer questions about family history of certain diseases, conditions, or disorders. This information falls under the definition of genetic information under the Genetic Information Nondiscrimination Act of 2008 (GINA, P.L. 110-233), and therefore its acquisition and use by employers is strictly protected and is protected differently than is acquisition of other medical information. Although GINA generally prohibits the acquisition of genetic information, it does allow for its collection as part of a wellness program, subject to certain requirements. As Congress considers the role that employer wellness programs may or can play in reforming the health care system, the potential interaction between GINA and any wellness program provisions is likely to be assessed.

This report provides an overview of GINA generally, a description of GINA's statutory exception allowing for the collection of genetic information pursuant to a wellness program, and a discussion of some of the key issues that either have arisen or may arise as lawmakers consider the role of these programs in health reform.

INTRODUCTION

Health reform is a major issue on the domestic policy agenda of the 111th Congress. Congress has been considering a number of policy proposals to reform the health delivery system that aim to improve health care quality, reduce health care costs, and expand access to care. A range of proposals have targeted reform of the delivery system through an increased focus on prevention and wellness in an effort to encourage individuals to adopt healthier lifestyles. One prominent policy lever being considered in some health delivery reform proposals is employer wellness programs. Employer wellness programs often focus on improving wellness overall, but may target a specific disease (e.g., diabetes) or behavior (e.g., smoking), may include the provision of a range of health or other services, and are offered by employers to employees through the workplace or other setting. These programs may include the provision of incentives for participation, ranging from additional paid time off to reduced insurance premium contributions.

Most if not all employer wellness programs collect medical information from participants. Programs may request or require participating employees to answer questions about family history of certain diseases, conditions, or disorders. This information falls under the definition of genetic information under the Genetic Information Nondiscrimination Act of 2008 (GINA), and therefore its acquisition and use by employers is strictly protected and is protected differently than is employer acquisition of other medical information.[1] Although GINA generally prohibits the acquisition of genetic information, it does allow for its collection as part of a wellness program, subject to certain requirements.

As Congress considers the role that employer wellness programs may or can play in reforming the health care system, the potential interaction between GINA and any wellness program provisions is likely to be assessed. Congress may, of course, enact legislation that may in effect or directly amend the requirements of GINA. This report provides an overview of GINA generally, a description of GINA's statutory exception allowing for the collection of genetic information pursuant to a wellness program, and a discussion of some of the key issues that either have arisen or may arise as lawmakers consider the role of these programs in health reform.[2]

Overview of the Genetic Information Nondiscrimination Act of 2008 (GINA)

On May 21, 2008, the Genetic Information Nondiscrimination Act of 2008 (GINA), referred to by its sponsors as the first civil rights act of the 21st century, was enacted. GINA, P.L. 110-233, prohibits discrimination by health insurers and employers based on genetic information. Genetic information is considered sensitive because it may be predictive and can affect not only an individual but also family members.[3]

GINA is divided into two main parts: Title I, which prohibits discrimination by health insurers based on genetic information, and Title II, which prohibits discrimination in employment based on genetic information. Title I of GINA amends the Employee Retirement Income Security Act of 1974 (ERISA), the Public Health Services Act (PHSA), and the Internal Revenue Code (IRC), through the Health Insurance Portability and Accountability Act of 1996 (HIPAA), as well as the Social Security Act, to prohibit health insurers from engaging in genetic discrimination and to strengthen and clarify existing HIPAA nondiscrimination and portability provisions. In this way, group plans under ERISA, group and individual plans under the PHSA, Church Plans under the IRC, and Medigap plans under the

SSA are all brought under the jurisdiction of the law. The complexity of the health care financing system required this multifaceted approach in order to ensure protection for all individuals, regardless of their coverage arrangement. On October 7, 2009, the Departments of Labor, Health and Human Services, and Treasury issued interim final regulations implementing the provisions in Title I of GINA. These regulations became effective as of December 7, 2009, and specifically for plan years beginning on or after December 7, 2009, for group health plans and health insurance issuers.[4]

Title II of GINA prohibits discrimination in employment because of genetic information and, with certain exceptions, prohibits an employer from requesting, requiring, or purchasing genetic information. The law prohibits the use of genetic information in employment decisions— including hiring, firing, job assignments, and promotions—by employers, unions, employment agencies, and labor management training programs. On March 2, 2009, the Equal Employment Opportunity Commission (EEOC) issued proposed regulations for Title II that generally closely track the statutory language.

GINA'S TITLE II EXCEPTION FOR EMPLOYER ACQUISITION OF GENETIC INFORMATION AS PART OF A WELLNESS PROGRAM

Although GINA broadly prohibits both the acquisition of genetic information, as well as the use of genetic information by employers in employment decisions, it does provide for several exceptions to the prohibition on employer acquisition of this information. Specifically, Title II of GINA allows employers, employment agencies, labor organizations, and training programs to acquire genetic information pursuant to the offering of health or genetic services, including services offered as part of a wellness program.[5] The statute states, in pertinent part, "(i)t shall be an unlawful employment practice for an employer to request, require, or purchase genetic information with respect to an employee or a family member of the employee except where health or genetic services are offered by the employer, including such services offered as part of a wellness program."[6] The exception provided for by this provision is materially identical for employment agencies, labor organizations, and training programs.

However, employers may collect genetic information as part of a wellness program, pursuant to this exception, *only* if they meet three requirements, as specified in statute. These include

- the employee must provide prior, knowing, voluntary and written authorization;
- only the employee and the licensed health care professional or board-certified genetic counselor involved in providing such services receive individually identifiable information concerning the results of such services; and
- any individually identifiable genetic information provided in connection with the health or genetic services provided under this exception is only available for the purposes of such services and shall not be disclosed to the employer except in aggregate terms that do not disclose the identity of specific employees.[7]

The EEOC's Notice of Proposed Rulemaking (NPRM), released on March 2, 2009, elaborates on these requirements. Specifically, it states that written authorization must (1) be written so that the individual from whom the genetic information is being obtained is reasonably likely to understand the form, (2) describe the type of genetic information that will be obtained and the general purposes for which it will be used, and (3) describe the restrictions on disclosure of genetic information.[8]

Importantly, regardless of how an employer may acquire genetic information (through these exceptions), the employer is still absolutely prohibited from using the information to discriminate in employment decisions, such as hiring, firing, and promotion.

Issues for Consideration

A number of issues arise with respect to the interaction between GINA and employer wellness programs. These include issues relating to the use of financial incentives for participation in wellness programs; what an employer may require of an employee in terms of either participation in wellness programs or provision of medical information pursuant to participation in wellness programs; and the relationship between GINA, underwriting, and financial incentives for participating in wellness programs.

Can an Employer Require an Employee to Participate in a Wellness Program under GINA?

GINA is silent on the issue of whether an employer may require participation in a wellness program (or if a wellness program may be mandatory). However, the Equal Employment Opportunity Commission (EEOC) Notice of Proposed Rulemaking (NPRM) states that "the proposed regulation reiterates the statutory provision [that a covered entity may offer health or genetic services], but further notes that a wellness program seeking medical information must be voluntary, which is a requirement set forth in the ADA."[9] In addition, the regulation refers to "voluntary wellness programs" when discussing allowed exceptions to the prohibition on employer acquisition of genetic information.

This is potentially an important issue with respect to the scope of the protections offered under GINA. If an employer were able to both require participation in a wellness program, and require the provision of certain medical and/or genetic information as part of the wellness program, this would in essence create a requirement that an employee share his or her genetic information with an employer. This would have the impact of limiting the scope of GINA's protections, as it would create an exception to the prohibition on an employer's acquisition of genetic information that would not be able to be mitigated by either employee choice or behavior. In addition, if both participation and provision of genetic information were able to be required, it would conflict with the statutory requirement under GINA that an employee provide *voluntary* written authorization for health or genetic services. If both were required by the employer, by definition, the employee could not provide voluntary written authorization for health or genetic services.

Can an Employer Require an Employee to Provide Genetic Information as Part of a Wellness Program under GINA?

As discussed above, an employer may not require that an employee participate in a wellness program (or accept health or genetic services) that requires the provision of medical information. However, an employer may require that, as a condition of participating in a voluntary wellness program, an employee provide certain medical and/or genetic information. This would comply with GINA's protections because if an employee did not want to divulge this information to his employer, he could opt to not participate in the wellness program. Of course, any provision of genetic information on the part of an employee, pursuant to participating in a wellness program, would still have to comply with the three statutory requirements set forth by GINA. The employee would have to provide voluntary, prior, and knowing written authorization; only the employee and the licensed health care professional or board-certified genetic counselor involved in providing the services could have access to individually identifiable information; and any individually identifiable information could not be disclosed to the employer except in aggregate terms that do not disclose the identity of specific employees.

It may appear that a requirement to provide genetic information pursuant to participation in a wellness program conflicts with GINA's requirement that an employee provide voluntary written authorization for health or genetic services. However, the written authorization would still be voluntary in as much as the employee would always have the option of not participating in the wellness program, and thus could voluntarily opt out of providing any genetic information to the employer.

Does GINA Preclude the Use of Financial Incentives to Encourage Participation in Wellness Programs?

Nothing in the statutory language of GINA would preclude the use of financial (or other) incentives by employers for participation in wellness programs. However, the EEOC NPRM notes that the definition of the term "voluntary," specifically with respect to financial incentives for participation in wellness programs, is not a settled matter. Specifically, it states that a wellness program is voluntary "as long as an employer neither requires participation nor penalizes employees who do not participate."[10] This suggests that it is possible that the interpretation may be made that a program could not be defined as voluntary if there are any financial incentives present at all (i.e., if a financial incentive for participation is interpreted as a penalty for not participating). However, it goes on to note that this definition has not been further developed and that comments on this specific point are invited.[11]

Advocates have expressed concern that the scope of GINA may be adversely affected if employers are allowed to offer any financial incentives for participation in wellness programs.[12] For example, the Council for Responsible Genetics maintains that wellness programs may be considered truly voluntary only if any incentives for participation are prohibited and if voluntary wellness programs are prohibited from requiring a health risk assessment.

In addition, it is possible that where an employer wellness program *requires* the provision of certain genetic information (e.g., family history of cancer or heart disease) that the literal effect of this could be to discourage participation by those individuals with certain family histories (i.e., genetic information). This may occur because, although GINA's protections are in place and discrimination based on genetic information is prohibited in employment and health insurance, individuals may not fully trust these protections and may prefer to keep that information private from their employer, rather than accrue the benefits of participation in the wellness program. Although this requirement is facially neutral it may in fact discourage the participation of individuals with certain family histories. Conversely, it is possible that individuals with a certain family history would prefer to take advantage of the services offered through a wellness program, and the potential for prevention, and would be more comfortable that the protections in place under GINA would protect them adequately.

Financial Incentives for Participation in a Wellness Program and Underwriting

Advocates have expressed concern that if an employer, who is also acting as an insurer, collects genetic information through a wellness program, and if these employers then adjust an employee's premium contribution based on participation in a wellness program, this may violate

GINA's prohibition on the use of genetic information for purposes of underwriting under Title I of the Act. Specifically, GINA provides that "a group health plan, and a health insurance issuer offering health insurance coverage in connection with a group health plan, shall not request, require, or purchase genetic information for underwriting purposes."[13] For purposes of Title I of the Act, the term "underwriting purposes" is defined as

> with respect to any group health plan, or health insurance coverage offered in connection with a group health plan—"(A) rules for, or determination of, eligibility (including enrollment and continued eligibility) for benefits under the plan or coverage; "(B) the computation of premium or contribution amounts under the plan or coverage; "(C) the application of any pre-existing condition exclusion under the plan or coverage; and "(D) other

> activities related to the creation, renewal, or replacement of a contract of health insurance or health benefits.[14]

The interim final regulations issued by the Departments of Labor, Health and Human Services, and Treasury clarify that the definition of "underwriting purposes" should be interpreted broadly to include activities outside the scope of those used for rating and pricing a group policy. Specifically, the regulation explains that the definition includes "changing deductibles or other cost-sharing mechanisms, or providing discounts, rebates, payments in kind, or other premium differential mechanisms in return for activities such as completing a health risk assessment (HRA) or participating in a wellness program."[15] Many HRAs collect family medical history, which falls under the scope of the definition of genetic information under GINA. For this reason, wellness plans administered by health plans or health insurance issuers that collect this information through HRAs, and that provide financial rewards for participation and for completion of the HRA, would be in violation of the statutory prohibition against the request of genetic information for underwriting purposes. Importantly, the violation is considered to be absolute, regardless of the amount of the financial award associated with the wellness program or whether the rewards are based directly on the outcome of the assessment.

There are certain circumstances under which a plan or issuer may either collect genetic information through an HRA *or* provide a financial incentive for participation in a wellness program or for completion of an HRA. In the first case, a plan or issuer may lawfully collect genetic information through an HRA if there is *no reward* to the enrollee associated with completing the HRA. In the second case, a plan or issuer may lawfully provide a financial incentive for participation in a wellness program or for completion of an HRA if the HRA does not collect any genetic information, including family history.

This regulatory determination raises several potentially consequential issues for consideration. First, it will most likely also affect the provision of services or collection of information through disease management programs, administered by a plan or issuer, and which include a financial incentive for participation. Second, it is possible that fewer plans and issuers will opt to offer wellness programs, or disease management programs, due to the increased cost of compliance for the plan and the restrictions on the type of information that may be collected in the context of a financial incentive. Additionally, if financial incentives are not offered, enrollees may be less inclined to participate in these programs. The combination of these two factors might result in a decrease in the early identification of disease, or its appropriate management, and a concomitant increase in morbidity and mortality as well as health care costs (accruing to both the payer and society broadly). And third, this may create a situation whereby certain employers—those who are also acting as health insurance issuers—will have to adhere to these requirements in terms of financial incentives for wellness programs, whereas others—those not acting in such a capacity— might be required to comply with different requirements relating to the provision of financial incentives and wellness programs, based on the EEOC's interpretation of this issue. The EEOC has not yet issued a final rule on Title II so it is not clear if the requirements will differ.

End Notes

[1] Title II of GINA defines genetic information as "with respect to any individual, information about such individual's genetic tests, the genetic tests of family members of such individual, and the manifestation of a disease or disorder in family members of such individual." P.L. 110-233, Section 201(4)(A).

[2] For a discussion of the legal issues relating to wellness programs, see CRS Report R40661, *Wellness Programs: Selected Legal Issues*, coordinated by Nancy Lee Jones.

[3] For more information about GINA, please see CRS Report RL34584, *The Genetic Information Nondiscrimination Act of 2008 (GINA)*, by Nancy Lee Jones and Amanda K. Sarata.

[4] 74 Fed. Reg. 51633 (October 7, 2009).

[5] P.L. 110-233. Section 202(b)(2), Section 203(b)(2), Section 204(b)(2), and Section 205(b)(2).

[6] P.L. 110-233. Section 202(b)(2)(A).

[7] P.L. 110-233. Section 202(b)(2)(B),(C), and (D).

[8] 74 *Federal Register* 9068 (March 2, 2009).

[9] 74 *Federal Register* 9062 (March 2, 2009).

[10] 74 *Federal Register* 9062 (March 2, 2009).

[11] HIPAA regulations address the issue of financial incentives and employer wellness programs. For more information about this issue, please see CRS Report R40661, *Wellness Programs: Selected Legal Issues*, coordinated by Nancy Lee Jones.

[12] Genetic Alliance Webinar, May 15, 2009. "Genetic Information Nondiscrimination Act: Title II (Employment)." Accessed at http://resourcerepository.org/documents/752/ ginaimplementation:titleii/#.

[13] P.L. 110-233. Section 101(b).

[14] P.L. 110-233. Section 101(d).

[15] 74 Fed. Reg. 51663 (October 7, 2009).

In: Genetic Information, Health Laws ... ISBN: 978-1-61942-176-9
Editors: Gossling and Richards

Chapter 3

WELLNESS PROGRAMS: SELECTED LEGAL ISSUES*

Nancy Lee Jones, Jody Feder, Edward C. Liu, Jennifer Staman, Kathleen S. Swendiman, and Jon O. Shimabukuro

SUMMARY

Health care costs have risen dramatically in recent years, and employers providing health insurance, as well as other insurance providers, have struggled to find ways to contain costs. This has led to the introduction of incentives to promote healthy behaviors, often referred to as wellness programs. These programs take a myriad of forms from providing a gym at the workplace to subsidizing the co-pays of certain medications and linking health care benefits or discounts to certain healthy lifestyles. In Arkansas, for example, state employees who exercise more frequently or eat healthier foods can earn up to three extra days off from work each year. These healthy lifestyle programs can include requirements for no tobacco use as well as requirements for certain cholesterol, blood pressure, or body mass index (BMI) measurements. For example, Scotts Miracle-Gro, a lawn care company, announced a policy that any smoking

* This is an edited, reformatted and augmented version of a Congressional Research Service publication, CRS Report for Congress R40661, from www.crs.gov, dated December 13, 2010.

by employees, whether on or off the job, would result in termination of employment.

There is a wide variety of wellness programs, and the application of existing law to a particular program is highly fact specific. One of the key distinctions is whether the health insurance program is provided by an individual's employer or whether it is provided by another source such as Medicaid. An employer-provided wellness program raises potential discrimination issues, since, if the employer obtains information about a health condition, there could be impacts not only on the provision of insurance but also on employment.

The health care reform law, the Patient Protection and Affordable Care Act of 2010 (PPACA, P.L. 111-148, as modified by the Health Care and Education Reconciliation Act, P.L. 111-152), significantly reformed the private health insurance market and included provisions on the implementation of employer wellness programs. This report will examine the legal issues raised by wellness programs, including discussions of PPACA, the Health Insurance Portability and Accountability Act (HIPAA) nondiscrimination rules, the Americans with Disabilities Act (ADA), the Genetic Information Nondiscrimination Act (GINA), other employment discrimination laws such as the Age Discrimination in Employment Act and Title VII of the Civil Rights Act of 1964, as well as Medicaid and applicable tax code provisions.

INTRODUCTION

Health care costs have risen dramatically in recent years,[1] and employers providing health insurance, as well as other insurance providers, have struggled to find ways to contain costs. This has led to the introduction of incentives to promote healthy behaviors, often referred to as wellness programs. These programs take a myriad of forms from providing a gym at the workplace to subsidizing the co-pays of certain medications and linking health care benefits or discounts to certain healthy lifestyles. In Arkansas, for example, state employees who exercise more frequently or eat healthier foods can earn up to three extra days off from work each year.[2] These healthy lifestyle programs can include requirements for no tobacco use as well as requirements for certain cholesterol, blood pressure, or body mass index (BMI) measurements.[3] For example, Scotts Miracle-Gro, a lawn care company, announced a policy that any smoking by employees, whether on or off the job, would result in termination of employment.[4]

There is a wide variety of wellness programs, and the application of existing law to a particular program is highly fact specific. One of the key distinctions is whether the health insurance program is provided by an individual's employer or whether it is provided by another source such as Medicaid. An employer-provided wellness program raises potential discrimination issues, since, if the employer obtains information about a health condition, there could be impacts not only on the provision of insurance but also on employment.

The health care reform law, the Patient Protection and Affordable Care Act of 2010 (PPACA, P.L. 111-148, as modified by the Health Care and Education Reconciliation Act, P.L. 111-152), significantly reformed the private health insurance market and included provisions on the implementation of employer wellness programs. This report will examine the legal issues raised by wellness programs, including discussions of PPACA, the Health Insurance Portability and Accountability Act (HIPAA) nondiscrimination rules, the Americans with Disabilities Act (ADA), the Genetic Information Nondiscrimination Act (GINA), other employment discrimination laws such as the Age Discrimination in Employment Act and Title VII of the Civil Rights Act of 1964, as well as Medicaid and applicable tax code provisions.[5]

Patient Protection and Affordable Care Act (PPACA)

PPACA, among other things, created a number of significant reforms to the private health insurance market.[6] These reforms include changes that will limit the ability of a group health plan or health insurance issuer to set premiums or determine eligibility for coverage based on criteria such as health status. PPACA also contains several provisions specifically relating to wellness programs.[7] These provisions include

- PPACA §1001, which creates a new §2717 in the Public Health Services Act (PHSA) concerning reporting requirements for group health plans;
- PPACA §1201, which creates a new §2705 in the PHSA prohibiting discrimination on the basis of health status;
- PPACA §4303, amended by §10404 of P.L. 111-152, creates sections in the PHSA, including section 399MM, which provides for Centers for Disease Control (CDC) technical assistance for employer-based wellness programs; and

- PPACA §10408, concerning workplace wellness grants.[8]

As discussed below, Section 1201 of PPACA in large part codified existing HIPAA wellness program regulations. The other three PPACA sections, PPACA §§1001, 4303, and 10408, all encourage the provision of wellness programs.

HEALTH INSURANCE PORTABILITY AND ACCOUNTABILITY ACT (HIPAA)[9]

Prior to the enactment of PPACA, Title I of the Health Insurance Portability and Accountability Act (HIPAA)[10] amended the Employee Retirement Income Security Act (ERISA),[11] the Public Health Service Act (PHSA), and the Internal Revenue Code (IRC) to improve portability and continuity of health coverage.[12] Among the provisions relating to health coverage, HIPAA established certain nondiscrimination requirements, which are intended to prevent group health plans[13] and group health insurance issuers[14] from discriminating against individual participants or beneficiaries based on a health factor. In particular, HIPAA prohibits a group health plan or health insurance issuer from basing coverage eligibility rules on health-related factors including health status (physical or mental), claims experience, receipt of health care, medical history, genetic information, evidence of insurability, or disability.[15] In addition, a group health plan or health insurance issuer may not require that an individual pay a higher premium or contribution than another "similarly situated"[16] participant, based on these health-related factors.[17] However, HIPAA contains an exception to this requirement, in that it "do[es] not prevent a group health plan and a health insurance issuer from establishing premium discounts or rebates or modifying otherwise applicable copayments or deductibles in return for adherence to programs of health promotion and disease prevention (i.e., wellness programs)."[18] On December 13, 2006, the Departments of Labor, Treasury, and Health and Human Services issued joint final regulations on the nondiscrimination provisions of HIPAA that provide a framework for structuring wellness programs.[19] The regulations explain that a group health plan or health insurance issuer may vary benefits, including cost-sharing mechanisms (such as a deductible, copayment, or coinsurance), based on whether an individual has met the requirements of a wellness program that satisfies various requirements.[20]

The regulations classify wellness programs into two basic types. First, if a wellness program provides incentives based solely on participation in a wellness program, or if the wellness program does not provide a reward, the program complies with HIPAA nondiscrimination requirements without having to satisfy any additional standards, as long as the program is made available to all similarly situated individuals.[21] Examples provided in the regulations include programs that reimburse all or part of the cost for memberships in a fitness center, reimburse employees for the costs of smoking cessation programs without regard to whether the employee quits smoking, or provide a reward to employees for attending a monthly health education seminar.[22]

However, if the conditions for obtaining a reward[23] under a wellness program are based on an individual meeting a certain standard relating to a health factor, then the program must meet five requirements as set forth in the HIPAA regulations.[24] First, the reward offered by this type of wellness program must not exceed 20% of the cost of employee coverage under the plan (i.e., the amount paid by the employer and the employee for that employee for coverage).[25] The agencies have indicated that this 20% limit is designed to avoid a reward or penalty being so large that is has the effect of denying coverage or creating a heavy financial penalty on individuals who do not satisfy an initial wellness program standard.[26] Second, the program must be "reasonably designed to promote health or prevent disease." Accordingly, a program satisfies this standard "if it has a reasonable chance of improving the health of or preventing disease in participating individuals and it is not overly burdensome, is not a subterfuge for discriminating based on a health factor, and is not highly suspect in the method chosen to promote health or prevent disease."[27] While the preamble to the final regulations explains that "bizarre, extreme, or illegal requirements" in a wellness program would be prohibited, it also states that there does not need to be a scientific record that the method used in the program promotes wellness. Thus, the "reasonably designed" standard is intended to allow diversity and experimentation in promoting wellness.[28]

Third, the program must give individuals eligible for the program the opportunity to qualify for the reward under the program at least once per year.[29] Fourth, the reward under the program must be available to all similarly situated individuals. As part of this requirement, a reasonable alternative standard (or waiver of the otherwise applicable standard) for obtaining the reward must be available for any individual for whom it is "unreasonably difficult" due to a medical condition to satisfy the otherwise applicable standard or it is "medically inadvisable" to attempt to satisfy the otherwise applicable standard.[30] While the regulations provide no guidance as to what constitutes "unreasonably difficult" or "medically inadvisable," a plan or issuer may seek verification, such as a statement from an individual's physician, that a health factor makes it unreasonably difficult or medically inadvisable for the individual to satisfy or attempt to satisfy the standard. Fifth, the plan must disclose in all plan materials describing the terms of the program the availability of a reasonable alternative standard (or the possibility of waiver of the otherwise applicable standard).

Effective for plan years beginning on or after January 1, 2014, PPACA generally codifies the HIPAA wellness program regulations.[31] Accordingly, wellness programs that do not require the satisfaction of a standard relating to a health factor and are made available to all similarly situated individuals are not considered discriminatory. If, however, a wellness program conditions receiving a reward (such as a premium rebate) on meeting a health factor-related standard, the program must meet the five requirements included in the HIPAA regulations, including a cap on the amount of the reward. However, PPACA specifies that the available reward under these programs must be capped at 30% of the cost of the employee-only coverage under the plan, as opposed to 20% under the HIPAA regulations. In addition, under PPACA, the Secretaries of HHS, Labor, and Treasury have the discretion to increase this reward to up to 50%.[32]

It should be noted that HIPAA's nondiscrimination requirements, as amended by PPACA, will only apply if the program is offered as part of a group health plan, or through an insurer that provides group health coverage.[33] Thus, programs offered outside of a group health plan as a separate employment policy would not be subject to HIPAA's requirements.[34] However, other federal laws (e.g., the ADA) may still apply to these programs.[35]

The Americans with Disabilities Act (ADA)[36]

Statutory Overview

The Americans with Disabilities Act (ADA)[37] is a broad civil rights act prohibiting discrimination against individuals with disabilities. As stated in the act, its purpose is "to provide a clear and comprehensive national mandate for the elimination of discrimination against individuals with disabilities."[38]

The threshold issue in any ADA case is whether the individual alleging discrimination is an individual with a disability. Several Supreme Court decisions have interpreted the definition of disability, generally limiting its application.[39] Since these Supreme Court interpretations, lower court decisions also interpreted the definition of disability strictly. Congress responded to these decisions by enacting the ADA Amendments Act, P.L. 110-325, which rejects the Supreme Court and lower court interpretations and amends the ADA to provide broader coverage.[40]

The ADA specifically covers employment. Title I of the ADA, as amended by the ADA Amendments Act of 2008, provides that no covered entity shall discriminate against a qualified individual on the basis of disability in regard to job application procedures; the hiring, advancement, or discharge of employees; employee compensation; job training; and other terms, conditions, and privileges of employment.[41] In addition, the ADA provides that the prohibition against discrimination includes medical examinations and inquiries.[42] Most significant for a discussion of wellness programs, the ADA contains specific limitations on pre-employment and post-employment inquiries. The ADA states in part that,

> A covered entity shall not require a medical examination and shall not make inquiries of an employee as to whether such employee is an individual with a disability or as to the nature or severity of the disability, unless such examination or inquiry is shown to be job-related and consistent with business necessity.... A covered entity may conduct voluntary medical examinations, including voluntary medical histories, which are part of an employee health program available to employees at that work site.[43]

Section 501 of the ADA addresses the application of the act to insurance. This section states that the ADA does not prohibit an insurer from "underwriting risks, classifying risks, or administering such risks that are based on or not inconsistent with State law" or "from establishing, sponsoring, observing or administering the terms of a bona fide benefit plan that are based on underwriting risks, classifying risks, or administering such risks that are based on or not inconsistent with State law."[44]

The ADA and Wellness Programs

The Definition of Disability

As was noted previously, the threshold issue in any ADA case is whether the individual alleging discrimination is an individual with a disability. Although there was significant regulatory and judicial interpretation of the original definition of disability in the ADA, the definition as amended by the ADA Amendments Act, P.L. 110-325, has not yet been the subject of judicial decisions and the EEOC has not yet promulgated final regulations.[45]

The language of the ADA Amendments Act and its legislative history both indicate that the definition of disability should be interpreted broadly. This could mean that obese individuals, those addicted to nicotine, or those with certain cholesterol or blood pressure measurements may be covered under the new language. Generally, such individuals had not been found to be covered under the previous definition of disability.[46] However, under the new definition, ADA issues may be raised by certain wellness programs targeting these conditions.

Legislative History and EEOC Guidance

Although, as noted above, the language of the ADA does not address wellness programs other than allowing voluntary medical examinations as part of an employment health program, its legislative history provides more guidance. The House Education and Labor Committee Report observes the following:

> A growing number of employers today are offering voluntary wellness programs in the workplace. These programs often include medical screening for high blood pressure, weight control, cancer detection, and the like. As long as the programs are voluntary and the medical records are maintained in a confidential manner and not used for the purpose of limiting health insurance eligibility or of preventing occupational advancement, these activities would fall within the purview of accepted activities.[47]

The Equal Employment Opportunity Commission (EEOC) issued guidance paralleling this legislative history and stating that an employer may make disability-related inquiries or conduct medical examinations as a part of a voluntary wellness program.[48] In its guidance, the EEOC emphasized that medical records acquired as part of the wellness program must be kept confidential and separate from personnel records and noted that "a wellness program is 'voluntary' as long as an employer neither requires participation nor penalizes employees who do not participate."[49]

The EEOC elaborated on the meaning of "voluntary" in a response to a letter asking whether a requirement that employees participate in a health risk assessment as a condition for participation in its health insurance plan violated the ADA.[50] The EEOC stated that "requiring that all employees take a health risk assessment that includes disability-related inquiries and medical examinations as a prerequisite for obtaining health insurance coverage does not appear to be job-related and consistent with business necessity, and therefore would violate the ADA."[51]

Observing that disability-related inquiries and medical examinations are permitted as part of a voluntary wellness program, the EEOC noted that the program described was not voluntary since if an employee did not participate in the health risk assessment, he or she would not be able to obtain insurance through the employer's plan. Interestingly, the EEOC had originally sent a letter stating that a wellness program would be considered voluntary as long as the inducement to participate in the program did not exceed 20% of the cost of employee coverage under the plan— the same percentage as provided in the HIPAA regulations before PPACA. Since the question posed to the EEOC had not raised the issue of what level of inducement might be permissible under the ADA, the EEOC withdrew that portion of the letter, noting "[t]he Commission is continuing to examine what level, if any, of financial inducement to participate in a wellness program would be permissible under the ADA."[52] It is uncertain, then, what level of inducement, if any, might be permitted under the ADA and if it would differ from that allowed under PPACA.

GENETIC INFORMATION NONDISCRIMINATION ACT (GINA)[53]

GINA, P.L. 110-233, prohibits discrimination based on genetic information by health insurers and employers.[54] GINA is divided into two main parts: Title I, which prohibits discrimination based on genetic information by health insurers; and Title II, which prohibits discrimination based on genetic information in employment. GINA specifically forbids an employer from requesting, requiring, or purchasing genetic information of an employee or a family member of an employee.[55] However, there are statutory exceptions relevant to wellness programs, which include:

> where – (A) health or genetic services are offered by the employer, including such services offered as part of a wellness program; (B) the employee provides prior, knowing, voluntary, and written authorization; (C) only the employee (or family member if the family member is receiving genetic services) and the licensed health care professional or board certified genetic counselor involved in providing such services receive individually identifiable information concerning the results of such services; and (D) any individually identifiable genetic information provided under subparagraph (C) in connection with the services provided under subparagraph (A) is only available for the purposes of such services and shall not be disclosed to the employer except in aggregate terms that do not disclose the identity of specific employees.[56]

Thus, in order to comply with GINA, any wellness program that collects genetic information must be voluntary, must be conditioned on written authorization, and must have strict privacy protections.

The EEOC regulations for Title II reiterate the exception and its requirements, elaborating on several of the statutory provisions.[57] For example, the regulations provide that written authorization may include authorization in an electronic format.[58] Similarly, the regulations provide restrictions on the disclosure of genetic information which restate the statutory requirement that any individually identifiable genetic information shall not be disclosed to the employer except in aggregate terms that do not disclose the identity of specific employees. The regulations clarify that GINA is not violated if the provider of the health services gives aggregated information to a covered entity that makes the genetic information of an individual readily identifiable without effort on covered entity's part. An example of this situation would be when there is a small number of participants.

In the proposed regulations, EEOC emphasized that wellness programs must be voluntary, and asked for comments concerning the appropriate level of inducement offered for participation in a wellness program. In the final regulations, the EEOC concluded that inducements may be offered to encourage individuals to participate in wellness programs but inducements may not be offered to provide genetic information. The EEOC provides the following example in the regulations as a situation that does not violate GINA.

> A covered entity offers $150 to employees who complete a health risk assessment with 100 questions, the last 20 of them concerning family medical history and other genetic information. The instructions for completing the health risk assessment make clear that the inducement will be provided to all employees who respond to the first 80 questions, whether or not the remaining 20 questions concerning family medical history and other genetic information are answered.[59]

However, if the health risk assessment does not make clear which questions must be answered, it would violate GINA.[60]

This is similar to the ADA in that the ADA also requires voluntary participation. However, unlike the ADA, GINA contains a specific requirement for a written authorization. It should be noted, though, that the ADA does contain requirements for medical examinations and inquiries.[61] The GINA regulations provide that the provisions relating to allowable financial inducements do not limit the rights or protections available under the ADA. Specifically, the GINA regulations note that "if an employer offers a financial inducement for participation in disease management programs or other programs that promote healthy lifestyles and/or require individuals to meet particular health goals, the employer must make reasonable accommodations to the extent required by the ADA...."[62]

OTHER EMPLOYMENT DISCRIMINATION LAWS[63]

In addition to the ADA and GINA, there are several other employment discrimination laws that employers may need to consider when implementing wellness programs, including the Age Discrimination in Employment Act (ADEA) and Title VII of the Civil Rights Act of 1964.

Age Discrimination in Employment Act (ADEA)

The ADEA prohibits employment discrimination against persons over the age of 40.[64] Under the statute, it is unlawful for an employer "to fail or refuse to hire or to discharge any individual or otherwise discriminate against any individual with respect to his compensation, terms, conditions, or privileges of employment, because of such individual's age."[65] The statute not only applies to hiring, discharge, and promotion, but also prohibits discrimination in employee benefit plans such as health coverage and pensions.

Because a wellness program would presumably constitute a health benefit for purposes of ADEA coverage, an ADEA violation may occur if a wellness program has a disparate impact on older employees. The ADEA has been held to authorize disparate impact claims, which arise when an otherwise neutral employment policy or practice has an adverse impact on a class of employees and is not otherwise reasonable.[66] Thus, if a wellness program establishes a health standard that is more difficult for older employees to achieve, it may create a disparate impact in violation of the statute.

Title VII of the Civil Rights Act of 1964

Title VII prohibits an employer from discriminating against any individual with respect to hiring or the terms and conditions of employment because of such individual's race, color, religion, sex, or national origin.[67] Because Title VII applies to a broad range of employment practices, discrimination regarding health benefits may also violate the act. Like the ADEA, Title VII prohibits employment practices that have a disparate impact on covered individuals.[68] As a result, if a wellness program establishes a health standard that is more difficult for members of the protected classes to achieve, it may create a disparate impact in violation of Title VII.

INTERNAL REVENUE CODE (IRC)[69]

Unlike the ADA or HIPAA, the IRC generally does not require or prohibit any particular conduct. Instead, it regulates private activity through the manipulation of financial incentives and disincentives in the form of an individual's tax liability. Legislative proposals to create new tax incentives for workplace wellness programs generally fall into two categories: (1) tax incentives for employees in the form of favorable tax treatment of employer-provided wellness benefits and (2) tax incentives, such as credits or deductions, to offset employers' costs inherent in establishing or maintaining a workplace wellness program.

Tax Treatment of Benefits Received by Employees

The benefits provided to an employee by a workplace wellness program may constitute taxable income under the IRC. The IRC computes the taxable income of a taxpayer by deducting certain amounts from a taxpayer's gross income. Gross income generally includes compensation provided in exchange for services.[70] This also includes amounts provided in a form other than cash.[71] Therefore, benefits provided by an employer exclusively to its employees through a wellness program would appear to presumptively be includable in the gross income of the employees.

Employees receiving workplace wellness benefits may attempt to rebut this presumption by arguing that those benefits should be excluded from gross income under IRC provisions such as those excluding gifts, employee achievement awards, fringe benefits, or health benefits provided by an employer. Whether or not a benefit qualifies as non-taxable income is likely to turn on factors other than any link to a workplace wellness program. In other words, the fact that a benefit is being provided as an incentive to promote an employee's health is unlikely to have any impact on whether the employee must ultimately pay taxes on the receipt of that benefit. Several tax provisions that may be relevant are discussed below. Importantly, this analysis only examines whether receipt of these benefits in the context of a workplace wellness program would constitute taxable income; other laws may prevent providing incentives or benefits in the manner described.

Gifts and Awards

Gifts are generally excluded from the recipient's gross income.[72] However, this provision explicitly does not apply to transfers from an employer to an employee.[73] Therefore, it would not be accurate to claim that a workplace wellness benefit, such as membership at an outside athletic facility or a retail gift certificate, could be excluded from an employee's gross income because it is a gift from the employer.

Prizes and awards are generally included in gross income.[74] However, the value of "employee achievement awards" are not included in the gross income of the recipient.[75] The IRS defines employee achievement awards narrowly, limiting application of this provision to awards given for length of service or safety.[76] It is unlikely that a wellness benefit could be construed as a "length of service" award, but to the extent that a wellness benefit or program could be construed as a "safety" award it may qualify for exclusion from a receiving employee's income.

Fringe Benefits

Fringe benefits received from an employer are excluded from an employee's gross income.[77] The IRC recognizes several types of fringe benefits including no-additional-cost services, qualified employee discounts, *de minimis* fringes, qualified transportation fringes, qualified moving expense fringes, qualified retirement planning services, and on-premises athletic facilities.[78]

Each fringe is subject to various limitations and requirements. For example, transit passes provided by an employer cannot exceed $120 per month (for tax years 2009 and on) in order to qualify as a transportation fringe.[79] Fringe benefits are not required to be provided to employees, nor are they required to be provided unconditionally. Not every workplace wellness benefit would qualify as a fringe benefit, but a workplace wellness program could offer fringe benefits (such as employee discounts or transit subsidies) as part of an incentive scheme to reward healthy behaviors without increasing employees' tax liability.

Employer-Provided Health Benefits

Amounts received by employees for medical care, and health insurance premiums provided by employers, under an employer-provided health plan are excluded from employees' gross income.[80] However, this exclusion only applies to amounts provided to the employee for medical care. The IRS has also promulgated regulations indicating that benefits which only promote general health do not qualify as "medical care" for these purposes.[81] Some workplace wellness benefits (such as high blood pressure screenings or vaccinations) might qualify as medical care because they serve a diagnostic or preventive function. On the other hand, other types of benefits (such as discounts on commercial gym memberships) might not qualify. Recipients of non-qualifying benefits would be required to include the value of those benefits in gross income, if they were provided in the context of an employer-provided health plan.

Cash Incentives

Health savings accounts (HSA) and health reimbursement accounts (HRA) can provide tax-advantaged accounts to pay for qualified medical expenses.[82] Among other benefits, employer contributions to HSAs and HRAs receive favorable tax treatment. Therefore, some have suggested that workplace wellness programs could include employer contributions to HSAs or HRAs as incentives without incurring additional tax liability on the part of the recipients.

While such a scheme may not increase a participating employee's tax liability, these arrangements may result in increased tax liability for employers in the form of excise taxes. Employer contributions to an HSA must be made comparably to participating employees; failure to satisfy this comparability requirement can subject an employer to an excise tax.[83] Similarly, group health plans, including HRAs, that engage in certain types of discrimination on the basis of health status may also be subject to excise taxes.[84]

Tax Treatment of Employers' Costs

An employer's costs in creating or administering a wellness program may currently be deducted from an employer's taxable income as a business expense, but other types of tax incentives have also been proposed to encourage employers to support wellness programs.[85] For example, in the 111th Congress, the Healthy Workforce Act would have provided a tax credit to businesses based on amounts expended to implement a qualifying wellness program.[86]

National Labor Relations Act[87]

The National Labor Relations Act (NLRA)[88] guarantees the right to engage in collective bargaining for most private-sector employees. Once a union has been designated as the exclusive bargaining representative for a bargaining unit, both the employer and the union have an obligation to negotiate with each other in good faith.[89] Section 8(d) of the NLRA directs the parties to "confer in good faith with respect to wages, hours, and other terms and conditions of employment."[90] The National Labor Relations Board and the courts have recognized a distinction between mandatory subjects of bargaining, which reflect the language in Section 8(d), and permissive subjects, which may be negotiated at the discretion of the parties.

Health benefits are generally considered to be a mandatory subject of bargaining.[91] A wellness program, depending on how it is structured and the kinds of benefits offered, may be considered similarly to be a mandatory subject of bargaining. Thus, in a unionized environment, it would be necessary to negotiate the implementation of such a program.

MEDICAID[92]

The Medicaid program, Title XIX of the Social Security Act, 42 U.S.C. 1396 *et seq.*, serves over 60 million people, and it provides health care services for some of the most vulnerable populations in the United States.[93] In an effort to improve beneficiaries' health and hold down health care costs, state Medicaid programs have increasingly emphasized prevention and wellness. To do this, states are using innovative design approaches and taking advantage of increased flexibility of federal requirements.

State public programs often serve as laboratories for testing innovative approaches to health care. Congress, in the Deficit Reduction Act of 2005, granted the states increased flexibility to use innovative approaches in their Medicaid programs to take care of the health care needs of their citizens. Data obtained from pilot or demonstration projects such as those described below can be used to help design future programs in both the public and private sectors to motivate persons to engage in healthy behaviors, improve their health, and hold down health care costs.[94]

New Flexibility under the Deficit Reduction Act of 2005

Traditionally, states have used the state plan waiver process authorized in Section 1115 of the Social Security Act, 42 U.S.C. § 1315, to alter their Medicaid programs to try out innovative ideas for health care coverage and delivery.[95] The waiver process is time-consuming and changes proposed through the waiver process must be budget neutral. In 2005, Congress enacted the Deficit Reduction Act of 2005 (DRA) which includes provisions making it easier for states to incorporate innovative ideas including wellness programs in their Medicaid plans without having to comply with budget neutrality requirements and going through the Section 1115 waiver process. Specifically, Section 6044 of P.L. 109-171 added a new Section 1937 to the Social Security Act allowing states to amend their Medicaid state plans to provide alternative benefit packages to beneficiaries, without regard to traditional Medicaid requirements such as comparability, statewideness, and freedom of choice. Because these changes are implemented as an amendment to the state's Medicaid plan, they do not require budget neutrality. These "benchmark plans," as they are called, include several coverage choices, as well as the option for a state to propose a plan that would have to be approved by the Department of Health and Human Services (HHS).[96]

While the DRA option provides more flexibility than the Section 1115 waiver process, there are still restrictions. Categories of individuals that can be required to enroll in an alternative Medicaid plan are generally limited to healthy adults and children. If benchmark coverage is provided to children, Early and Periodic Screening, Diagnostic and Treatment (EPSDT) services must continue to be provided to individuals under age 21. These services include comprehensive screening services (i.e., well-child visits, immunizations) as well as dental, vision, and hearing services. In addition, EPSDT guarantees access to all federally coverable services necessary to treat an identified problem or condition among eligibles.[97]

The West Virginia Pilot Program

West Virginia, one of the first states to receive approval for a DRA State Plan Amendment establishing alternative benefits, began a pilot program in 2006 offering certain Medicaid enrollees a choice of two benefit packages—a basic plan and an enhanced plan that included benefits not traditionally offered under Medicaid.[98] What sets this concept apart from other wellness programs is the fact that the enhanced plan requires the beneficiary to adhere to an agreement or else lose access to additional health benefits such as substance abuse and mental health services.[99]

West Virginia's basic plan includes all mandatory Medicaid services. The enhanced plan provides all mandatory Medicaid services with additional optional services including wellness benefits such as tobacco cessation services, nutritional education, diabetes care, and chemical dependency and mental health services. The enhanced plan also includes skilled nursing care and orthotics/prosthetics for children. In order to enroll in the enhanced benefit plan, beneficiaries must sign an agreement stating that they will comply with all recommended medical treatment and wellness behaviors.[100] These include keeping medical appointments, getting recommended medical screenings, avoiding unnecessary emergency room visits, and taking prescribed medications. Physicians and managed care organizations monitor members' adherence to the member agreement and report to the state if the agreement is not met. If members are found not to be meeting their responsibilities, they are placed back into the Basic Medicaid plan. The West Virginia Medicaid website describes the state's "Mountain Health Choices" program as follows:

> Mountain Health Choices gives members a choice of benefit plans, requires responsibility, sets expectations for behavior and rewards success. It is designed to encourage healthy habits for all West Virginia Medicaid

> members. Medicaid members who sign the Member Responsibility Agreement will have access to services not provided in traditional Medicaid Benefits. By visiting their medical home for a check-up and working with their healthcare providers to set goals for health improvement, members qualify for the Enhanced Benefit Package. This package provides the opportunity for members to participate in weight management, physical activity and other educational opportunities for health improvement. Members who choose not to sign the Member Responsibility Agreement will have the Basic Benefit Package. This package covers all healthcare services which are mandated by federal and state laws. Medicaid members will have the opportunity to enroll in the Enhanced Benefit Package each year upon their date of re-determination and for 90 days after that date.[101]

Other State Medicaid Wellness Initiatives

Using the DRA flexibility and the ability to apply for Section 1115 waivers, other states have also implemented innovations aimed at engaging Medicaid beneficiaries in prevention and wellness programs. Some states are rewarding their Medicaid recipients for participating in wellness activities, such as disease management, smoking cessation, or weight loss programs. The rewards may be in the form of additional benefits not otherwise offered as part of the plan, or in the form of points to be used toward additional wellness activities. For example, in Idaho, Medicaid beneficiaries pay a monthly premium up to $15 per member. Beneficiaries can earn 30 points every three months by receiving recommended wellness visits and by keeping immunizations up-to-date. Each point equals $1 which can be used to offset premium payments.[102] Florida's Medicaid program includes innovations obtained through a Section 1115 waiver. These consumer engagement provisions include enhanced benefits accounts, which offer credits for enrollees who maintain healthy behaviors.[103] Beneficiaries may use the credits for up to three years after leaving the Medicaid program, thus providing a transition out of Medicaid coverage. The credits can be used to buy things like over-the-counter medications and nutritional and smoking cessation classes.[104] Under the DRA provisions, Wisconsin has implemented pay-for-performance incentives for its BadgerCare Plus managed care programs to increase member participation in prevention and wellness programs. Plans will receive an incentive reward for increasing the percentage of smokers they help quit the habit through participation in a tobacco cessation initiative. Plans can also receive an incentive reward for increasing the percentage of members who receive appropriate dental care, and for children under 21 who receive a free health checkup that is offered.[105]

End Notes

[1] For a discussion of the health costs of chronic diseases, see http://www.cdc.gov/NCCdphp/overview.htm.

[2] National Conference of State Legislatures, *State Employee Health Benefits* (Updated February 28, 2010).

[3] For a discussion of these types of wellness programs, see Lucinda Jesson, "Weighing the Wellness Programs: The Legal Implications of Imposing Personal Responsibility Obligations," 15 Va. J. Soc. Policy and Law 217 (2008). 4 *Id.*

[5] State statutes, such as smokers' rights laws, are beyond the scope of this report. One commentator has noted that 27 states and the District of Columbia prohibit employment discrimination based on smoking while not on the job. See Lucinda Jesson, "Weighing the Wellness Programs: The Legal Implications of Imposing Personal Responsibility Obligations," 15 Va. J. Soc. Policy and Law 217 (2008).

[6] For a more detailed discussion of PPACA see CRS Report R40942, *Private Health Insurance Provisions in the Patient Protection and Affordable Care Act (PPACA)*, by Hinda Chaikind, Bernadette Fernandez, and Mark Newsom.

[7] For a more detailed discussion of these provisions, see CRS Report R40943, *Public Health, Workforce, Quality, and Related Provisions in the Patient Protection and Affordable Care Act (P.L. 111-148)*, coordinated by C. Stephen Redhead and Erin D. Williams.

[8] For a discussion of all the PPACA provisions relating to prevention and wellness, see CRS Report R40943, *Public Health, Workforce, Quality, and Related Provisions in the Patient Protection and Affordable Care Act (P.L. 111-148)*, coordinated by C. Stephen Redhead and Erin D. Williams.

[9] This section was written by Jennifer Staman.

[10] P.L. 104-191, 110 Stat. 1936 (Aug. 21, 1996).

[11] While not addressed in this report, ERISA may affect the operation of wellness programs, aside from the provisions discussed in this section. For example, ERISA imposes certain obligations on plan fiduciaries, persons who are generally responsible for the management and operation of employee benefit plans. See 29 U.S.C. § 1101 *et seq*. In addition, ERISA contains a remedial scheme under which participants and beneficiaries may be able to bring suit for certain ERISA violations. See 29 U.S.C. § 1132(a). If a wellness program is offered as part of a group health plan under ERISA, then these sections of ERISA may apply to the programs. For a general discussion of ERISA, see CRS Report RL34443, *Summary of the Employee Retirement Income Security Act (ERISA)*, by Patrick Purcell and Jennifer Staman.

[12] It is important to note that the provisions of ERISA, the PHSA, and the IRC cover different health plans. In general, while ERISA covers private-sector employee benefit plans and health insurance issuers, it does not cover governmental plans, church plans, or plans with fewer than two participants. The PHSA covers both group health plans and health insurance issuers in the group and the individual market, as well as some governmental plans. The IRC covers group health plans, including church plans, but does not cover health insurance issuers.

[13] A group health plan is defined by ERISA and the PHSA as a plan established or maintained by an employer, to the extent that the plan provides medical care to employees or their dependents directly or through insurance, reimbursement, or otherwise. See 29 U.S.C. § 1191b(a); 42 U.S.C. § 300gg-91(a). Under the IRC, the definition of group health plan means a plan (including a self-insured plan) of, or contributed to by, an employer or employee organization to provide health care to the employees, former employees, the

employer, others associated or formerly associated with the employer in a business relationship, or their families. 26 U.S.C. § 5000(b)(1).

[14] In general, a health insurance issuer means an insurance company, insurance service, or insurance organization which is licensed to engage in the business of insurance in a state and which is subject to state law which regulates insurance. 29 U.S.C. § 1191b(b)(2); 42 U.S.C. § 300gg-91(b)(2).

[15] 29 U.S.C. § 1182(a); 42 U.S.C. § 300gg-1(a); 26 U.S.C. § 9802(a). The regulations also establish that group health plans and health insurance issuers may establish more favorable rules for eligibility for individuals with an adverse health factor, practice referred to as benign discrimination. 29 C.F.R. § 2590.702(g); 45 C.F.R. § 146.121(g); 26 C.F.R. § 54.9802-1(g).

[16] The HIPAA regulations do not define the term "similarly situated," but do permit a plan or issuer to treat participants as two or more distinct groups of similarly situated individuals if the distinction is based on a "bona fide employmentbased classification consistent with the employer's usual business practice." Bona fide classifications can include fulltime versus part-time status, geographic location, membership in a collective bargaining unit, date of hire, length of service, current employee versus former employee status, and different occupations. See 29 C.F.R. § 2590.702(d)(1); 45 C.F.R. § 146.121(d)(1); 26 C.F.R. § 54.9802-1(d)(1). 17 29 U.S.C. § 1182(b)(1); 42 U.S.C. § 300gg-1(b)(1); 26 U.S.C. § 9802(b)(1). It should be noted that the IRC does not apply to health insurance issuers.

[18] 29 U.S.C. § 1182(b)(2)(B); 42 USC 300gg-1(b)(2)(B); 26 U.S.C. § 9802(b)(2)(B).

[19] Nondiscrimination and Wellness Programs in Health Coverage in the Group Market, 71 Fed. Reg. 75014 (Dec. 13, 2006).

[20] 29 C.F.R. § 2590.702(b)(1)(ii); 45 C.F.R. 146.121(b)(1)(ii); 26 C.F.R. § 54.9802-1(b)(1)(ii).

[21] 29 C.F.R. § 2590.702(f)(1); 45 C.F.R. § 146.121(f)(1); 26 C.F.R. § 54.9802-1(f)(1).

[22] *Id.*

[23] The regulations provide that a reward can take the form of a discount or rebate of a premium or contribution, a waiver of all or part of a cost-sharing mechanism (e.g., deductibles, copayments, or coinsurance), the absence of a surcharge, or the value of a benefit that would otherwise not be provided under the plan (e.g., a prize). 29 C.F.R. § 2590.702(f)(2)(i); 45 C.F.R. § 146.121(f)(2)(i); 26 C.F.R. § 54.9802-1(f)(2)(i).

[24] To illustrate the distinction between the two types of wellness programs under the HIPAA regulations, a program that reimburses similarly situated individuals for a gym membership need not meet any additional requirements. Alternatively, a program that reimburses the cost of a gym membership if a certain weight loss goal is achieved must meet the additional five factors. See Susan Relland, *Legal Compliance for Wellness Programs*, Employee Benefit Plan Review (Mar. 2008).

[25] In addition to employees, if dependents (such as spouses or spouses and dependent children) participate in the wellness program, the reward must not exceed 20 percent of the cost of the coverage in which an employee and any dependents are enrolled. The cost of coverage is determined based on the total amount of contributions made by both the employer and the employee for the benefit package under which the employee and any dependents receive coverage. 29 C.F.R. § 2590.702(f)(2)(i); 45 C.F.R. § 146.121(f)(2)(i); 26 C.F.R. § 54.9802-1(f)(2)(i).

[26] 71 Fed. Reg. at 75018.

[27] The preamble to the final regulations provides that a program may fail to meet the "reasonable design" requirement if it imposes, as a condition of obtaining the reward, an overly burdensome time commitment or a requirement to engage in illegal behavior. *Id.*

[28] As an example, the preamble states that a plan or issuer could satisfy the "reasonably designed" standard by providing rewards to individuals who participated in a course of aromatherapy. *Id.*

[29] 29 C.F.R. § 2590.702(f)(2)(iii); 45 C.F.R. § 146.121(f)(2)(iii); 26 C.F.R. § 54.9802-1(f)(2)(iii).

[30] 29 C.F.R. § 2590.702(f)(2)(iv); 45 C.F.R. § 146.121(f)(2)(iv); 26 C.F.R. § 54.9802-1(f)(2)(iv).

[31] P.L. 111-148, § 1201 (creating section 2705 of the PHSA).

[32] The increase in the amount of the reward available has been lauded by some as encouraging behavioral change that will lead to improved health and lower costs. See Michael O'Donnell, "Integrating Financial Incentive for Workplace Health Promotion Programs into Health Plan Premiums is the Best Idea Since Sliced Bread," 24 AMERICAN JOURNAL OF HEALTH PROMOTION iv (March/April 2010). However, others have argued that tying premium discounts to achieving certain health standards shifts costs to less healthy individuals who tend to be those with lower incomes. See Roni Caryn Rabin, "Could Health Overall Incentives Hurt Some?" THE NEW YORK TIMES (April 12, 2010); http://www.nytimes.com/2010/04/13/health/13land.html.

[33] It should be noted that PPACA would also require the HHS Secretary, in consultation with the Secretaries of the Treasury and Labor, to establish a 10-state pilot program in which participating states would be required to apply the wellness program provisions to health insurers in the individual market.

[34] Department of Labor Field Assistance Bulletin 2008-02 (Feb. 14, 2008), available at http://www.dol.gov/ebsa/pdf/fab2008-2.pdf.

[35] Id.

[36] This section was written by Nancy Jones.

[37] 42 U.S.C. §§12101 *et seq*. For a more detailed discussion of the ADA, see CRS Report 98-921, *The Americans with Disabilities Act (ADA): Statutory Language and Recent Issues*, by Nancy Lee Jones.

[38] 42 U.S.C. §12101(b)(1).

[39] *Sutton v. United Air Lines, Inc.*, 527 U.S. 471 (1999); *Murphy v. United Parcel Service, Inc.*, 527 U.S. 516 (1999); *Kirkingburg v. Albertson's Inc.*, 527 U.S. 555 (1999); *Toyota Motor Manufacturing v. Williams*, 534 U.S. 184 (2002).

[40] For a discussion of the ADA Amendments Act, see CRS Report RL34691, *The ADA Amendments Act: P.L. 110-325*, by Nancy Lee Jones.

[41] 42 U.S.C. §12112(a), as amended by P.L. 110-325, §5.

[42] 42 U.S.C. §12112(d)

[43] 42 U.S.C. §12112(d)(4).

[44] 42 U.S.C. §12201(c).

[45] Proposed regulations were published in the Federal Register on September 23, 2009. 74 FED. REG. 48431 (Sept. 23, 2009). For a discussion of these regulations see CRS Report R40875, *The Americans with Disabilities Act (ADA): Proposed Employment Regulations*, by Nancy Lee Jones.

[46] For a discussion of ADA cases on obesity prior to enactment of the ADA Amendments Act, see CRS Report RS22609, *Obesity Discrimination and the Americans with Disabilities Act*, by Jennifer Staman.

[47] H.Rept. 101-485, pt. 2, at 75 (1990).

[48] http://www.eeoc.gov/policy/docs/guidance-inquiries.html#10.

[49] *Id.*

[50] http://www.eeoc.gov/foia/letters/2009/ada_disability_medexam_healthrisk.html.

[51] *Id.*

[52] *Id.*

[53] This section was written by Nancy Jones.

[54] For a discussion of GINA generally, see CRS Report RL34584, *The Genetic Information Nondiscrimination Act of 2008 (GINA)*, by Nancy Lee Jones and Amanda K. Sarata. For a more detailed discussion of GINA and wellness programs see CRS Report R41314, *The Genetic Information Nondiscrimination Act of 2008 and the Patient Protection and Affordable Care Act of 2010: Overview and Legal Analysis of Potential Interactions*, coordinated by Amanda K. Sarata, and CRS Report R40791, *Employer Wellness Programs: Health Reform and the Genetic Information Nondiscrimination Act*, by Amanda K. Sarata.

[55] 42 U.S.C. §2000ff-1(b). Identical requirements, including the statutory exceptions, are placed on employment agencies [42 U.S.C. §2000ff-2(b)], labor organizations [42 U.S.C. §2000ff-3(b)], and training programs [42 U.S.C. §2000ff-4(b)].

[56] 42 U.S.C. §2000ff-1(b)(2).

[57] 29 C.F.R. §1635.8(b)(2), 75 FED. REG. 68935 (November 9, 2010). For a discussion of the EEOC's Title II regulations under GINA see CRS Report R41527, *The Genetic Information Nondiscrimination Act (GINA): Final Employment Regulations*, by Nancy Lee Jones.

[58] 29 C.F.R. §1635.8(b)(2)(i)(B), 75 FED. REG. 68935 (November 9, 2010).

[59] 29 C.F.R. §1635.8(b)(2)(ii)(A), 75 FED. REG. 68935 (November 9, 2010).

[60] 29 C.F.R. §1635.8(b)(2)(ii)(B), 75 FED. REG. 68935 (November 9, 2010).

[61] 42 U.S.C. 12112(d).

[62] 29 C.F.R. §1635.8(b)(2)(iv), 75 FED. REG. 68936 (November 9, 2010).

[63] This section was written by Jody Feder.

[64] 29 U.S.C. §§ 621 et seq.

[65] Id. at § 623.

[66] Smith v. City of Jackson, 544 U.S. 228 (2005).

[67] 42 U.S.C. § 2000e-2.

[68] Id. *See also*, Griggs v. Duke Power Co., 401 U.S. 424 (1971).

[69] This section was written by Edward Liu.

[70] 26 U.S.C. § 61(a)(1).

[71] Treas. Reg. § 1.61-2(d).

[72] 26 U.S.C. § 102(a).

[73] 26 U.S.C. § 102(c).

[74] 26 U.S.C. § 74(a).

[75] 26 U.S.C. § 74(c)(1).

[76] 26 U.S.C. § 274(j)(3)(A).

[77] 26 U.S.C. § 132.

[78] *Id.*

[79] 26 U.S.C. § 132(f)(2)(A); Rev. Proc. 2008-66, § 3.12.

[80] 26 U.S.C. §§ 105(b), 106.

[81] Treas. Reg. § 1.213(e)(1)(ii). "An expenditure which is merely beneficial to the *general health* of an individual, such as an expenditure for a vacation, is not an expenditure for medical care."

[82] 26 U.S.C. § 223. *See also* CRS Report RS21573, *Tax-Advantaged Accounts for Health Care Expenses: Side-by-Side Comparison*, by Carol Rapaport.

[83] *See* 26 U.S.C. § 4980G. Therefore, if an employer provides HSA contributions only to those employees that meet certain wellness goals, it may be subject to an excise tax.

[84] *See* 26 U.S.C. §§ 4980D, 9802. Among the types of prohibited discrimination are those prohibited by HIPAA and GINA discussed *supra*.

[85] 26 U.S.C. § 162(a).

[86] H.R. 1897 and S. 803. Under either bill, a qualifying wellness program would be required to contain components addressing at least three of the following: health awareness, employee engagement, behavioral change, or a supportive environment.

[87] This section was written by Jon Shimabukuro.

[88] 29 U.S.C. § 151 *et seq*.

[89] *See* 29 U.S.C. § 158(a)(5), (b)(3) (making it an unfair labor practice to refuse to bargain collectively with the exclusive representative of a bargaining unit or an employer).

[90] 29 U.S.C. § 158(d).

[91] *See* The Developing Labor Law 1274-81 (John E. Higgins et al. eds., 2006).

[92] This section was written by Kathleen Swendiman.

[93] Centers for Medicare and Medicaid, 2008 Date Compendium at http://www.cms.hhs.gov/DataCompendium/01_Overview.asp#TopOfPage.

[94] G. Bishop and A. C. Brodkey, Personal Responsibility and Physician Responsibility—West Virginia's Medicaid Plan, *New England Journal of Medicine,* August 24, 2006, 355 (8): 756; Pat Redmond, Judith Solomon, and Mark Lin, *Can Incentives for Health Behavior Improve Health and Hold Down Medicaid Costs?* (Washington: Center on Budget and Policy Priorities, June 2007); Issue Brief, *Medicaid Redesigned: State Innovations in Health Coverage and Delivery,* National Governors' Association Center for Best Practices, March 27, 2008.

[95] The Section 1115 waiver process has been used by states for such purposes as expanding covered populations, incorporating new services, or using innovative delivery systems. See Medicaid State Waiver Program Demonstration Projects – General Information, Centers for Medicare and Medicaid Services, http://www.cms.hhs.gov/MedicaidStWaivProgDemoPGI/.

[96] Section 1937(b) of the Social Security Act, 42 U.S.C. § 1396u-7(b).

[97] EPSDT benefits are fairly broad sets of services provided to Medicaid children, 42 U.S.C. § 1396a(a)(43), 42 U.S.C. § 1396d(r).

[98] See also HHS Press Release, "HHS Approves Innovative Medicaid Reform in West Virginia," at http://www.hhs.gov/news/press/2006pres/20060503.html.

[99] Concerns have been raised about this and other Medicaid wellness "reward/penalty" plans, including whether the plans' requirements address the various barriers low income individuals face in reaching health goals, e.g., lack of child care or transportation services needed to attend exercise classes or nutrition counseling. See *Reward/Penalty Plans for Wellness: Coming Soon to an Office Near You?* Families USA (February 2008).

[100] http://www.wvdhhr.org/bms/oAdministration/Medicaid_Redesign/redesign_Member Agreement.pdf.

[101] ttp://www.wvdhhr.org/bms/oAdministration/Medicaid_Redesign/MedRedesign_main.asp.A recent report on the effectiveness of West Virginia's Mountain Health Choices program may be viewed at http://www.hsc.wvu.edu/wvhealthpolicy/reports/RWJ% 20Policy%20Brief%0FINAL%2003.27.09.pdf.

[102] *See* Idaho's Preventative Health Assistance program under Medicaid at http://www.healthandwelfare.idaho.gov/Medical/Medicaid/PreventiveHealthAssistance/tabid/221/Default.aspx. A June 2010 report on the effectiveness of Idaho's Medicaid wellness programs may be viewed at http://www.shadac.org/files/shadac/publications/ IdahoMedicaidDRACaseStudy.pdf.

[103] *Introducing the Enhanced Benefits Account Program* (Florida: Florida Agency for Health Care Administration, August 2007) at http://ahca.myflorida.com/Medicaid/Enhanced_Benefits/index.shtml. See, also, John Barth and Jessica Greene, *Encouraging Healthy*

Behaviors in Medicaid: Early Lessons from Florida and Idaho (Issue Brief, Center for Health Care Strategies, Inc. July 2007), available at http://www.chcs.org/usr_doc/Encouraging_Healthy_Behaviors_in_Medicaid.pdf.

[104] Studies are starting to be published regarding the effectiveness of these new programs. For example, see "Florida's Experience with Medicaid Reform: *The Enhanced Benefits Rewards Program: Is it changing the way Medicaid beneficiaries approach their health?*" (Georgetown University Health Policy Institute: Briefing #6), July 2008, available at http://ihcrp.georgetown.edu/floridamedicaid/pdfs/briefing6.pdf.

[105] Louise Kertesz, Renewed Focus on Prevention and Wellness in State Medicaid Programs, *AHIP Coverage,* October 10, 2008 at 2. *See* Wisconsin BadgerCare Plus Home Page at http://www.badgercareplus.org/.

In: Genetic Information, Health Laws ... ISBN: 978-1-61942-176-9
Editors: Gossling and Richards

Chapter 4

THE GENETIC INFORMATION NONDISCRIMINATION ACT (GINA): FINAL EMPLOYMENT REGULATIONS*

Nancy Lee Jones

SUMMARY

The Genetic Information Nondiscrimination Act of 2008 (GINA) prohibits discrimination based on genetic information by health insurers and employers. GINA is divided into two main parts: Title I, which prohibits discrimination based on genetic information by health insurers; and Title II, which prohibits discrimination in employment based on genetic information. Title II of GINA prohibits discrimination in employment because of genetic information and, with certain exceptions, prohibits an employer from requesting, requiring, or purchasing genetic information. The law prohibits the use of genetic information in employment decisions—including hiring, firing, job assignments, and promotions—by employers, unions, employment agencies, and labor management training programs and mandates confidential treatment of any genetic information that is obtained.

The Equal Employment Opportunity Commission (EEOC) promulgated final regulations under Title II of GINA on November 9,

* This is an edited, reformatted and augmented version of a Congressional Research Service publication, CRS Report for Congress R41527, from www.crs.gov, dated December 9, 2010.

2010. The EEOC noted that the regulations closely track the statutory language but they do provide clarification regarding definitions in GINA; provide guidance regarding the exceptions in GINA to employer liability for acquiring genetic information; discuss the application of GINA to wellness programs; and discuss the interplay between GINA and other statutes. The regulations also provide specific examples to help clarify the requirements of the statute and regulations. For instance, the regulations clarify that a genetic test includes a test to determine whether an individual has a BRCA1 or BRCA2 variant which would indicate a predisposition to breast cancer, and would include preimplantation genetic diagnosis in embryos. The regulations also specifically state that a test for cholesterol levels is not a genetic test. Similarly, the regulations provide a definition of manifested disease, and note that when the diagnosis of a disease depends on both signs and symptoms and genetic information, the disease will be considered manifested. It was emphasized, however, that medical information is still subject to other laws, such as Title I of the Americans with Disabilities Act (ADA), which regulates the acquisition and use of medical information.

GINA and its regulations prohibit the collection of genetic information by employers but do provide some exceptions. The question of how the EEOC would interpret GINA's application to employer-run wellness programs was highly anticipated. In the final regulations, the EEOC concluded that inducements may be offered to encourage individuals to participate in wellness programs, but inducements may not be offered to provide genetic information. However, the EEOC does not permit a covered entity to request genetic information in order to evaluate whether an employee or applicant is able to safely and effectively perform the job. This is in contrast to the ADA as interpreted by the Supreme Court in Chevron v. Echazabal, where the Court found no violation of the ADA when an employer refused to hire an individual whose health would be endangered by the job. This issue may become more problematic as genetic information becomes more widely used.

Generally, the EEOC GINA regulations provide significant guidance to employers, especially in the use of examples, and in the clarification of GINA's applicability to wellness programs. However, due to the lack of decided cases and the ever-changing science, there is still some uncertainty concerning GINA's exact parameters.

INTRODUCTION

The Genetic Information Nondiscrimination Act of 2008 (GINA),[1] referred to by its sponsors as the first civil rights act of the 21st century, was enacted on May 21, 2008.[2] GINA, P.L. 110-233, prohibits discrimination based on genetic information by health insurers and employers. The sequencing of the human genome and subsequent advances raise hope for genetic therapies to cure disease, but this scientific accomplishment is not without potential problems.[3] An employer or health insurer could decide to take adverse action based on a genetic predisposition to disease, and situations have arisen where discriminatory action based on genetic information may have occurred.[4] In addition, there is evidence that the fear of genetic discrimination has an adverse effect on those seeking genetic testing, as well as on participation in genetic research.[5] GINA was enacted to remedy these situations.

GINA is divided into two main parts: Title I, which prohibits discrimination based on genetic information by health insurers; and Title II, which prohibits discrimination in employment based on genetic information. Title I of GINA amends the Employee Retirement Income Security Act of 1974 (ERISA), the Public Health Service Act (PHSA), and the Internal Revenue Code (IRC), through the Health Insurance Portability and Accountability Act of 1996 (HIPAA), as well as the Social Security Act, to prohibit health insurers from engaging in genetic discrimination.[6] Title II of GINA prohibits discrimination in employment because of genetic information and, with certain exceptions, prohibits an employer from requesting, requiring, or purchasing genetic information. The law prohibits the use of genetic information in employment decisions—including hiring, firing, job assignments, and promotions—by employers, unions, employment agencies, and labor management training programs.

The Equal Employment Opportunity Commission (EEOC) promulgated final regulations under Title II of GINA on November 9, 2010. These regulations take effect on January 10, 2011, 60 days after publication in the Federal Register.[7] The EEOC noted that the regulations closely track the statutory language. However, they do provide clarification regarding definitions in GINA; provide guidance regarding the exceptions in GINA to employer liability for acquiring genetic information; discuss the application of GINA to wellness programs; and discuss the interplay between GINA and other statutes. The regulations also provide specific examples to help clarify the requirements of the statute and regulations. This report examines the final EEOC Title II regulations with an emphasis on areas where the regulations elaborate upon the statutory requirements.

DEFINITIONS

Overview

Generally, the definitions in the final regulations track the statutory definitions although where the statute incorporates the provisions of other statutes, such as Title VII of the Civil Rights Act, the final GINA regulations specifically describe the provisions incorporated. In addition, the regulations include a definition of "covered entity," which the EEOC describes as "a simplifying shorthand to aid in the readability of the final regulation...."[8] Title II of GINA covers employers, unions, employment agencies, and labor management training programs, and rather than reiterating this coverage, where appropriate the regulations refer to "covered entity." Although the use of "covered entity" was criticized in the proposed regulations because of possible confusion with the Health Insurance Portability and Accountability Act (HIPPA), the EEOC kept the term in the final regulations noting that, since most of the entities subject to Title II of GINA are not HIPAA covered entities, there should be no confusion.[9] The following discussion covers several of the most significant regulatory definitions, and does not discuss those that largely track the statutory language.

Employee

An employee is defined in the regulations, in part, as "an individual employed by a covered entity, as well as an applicant for employment and a former employee."[10] The inclusion of former employees in the proposed regulations was controversial,[11] but the EEOC kept the language, noting that the Supreme Court in *Robinson v. Shell Oil Company*[12] stated that the definition of employee in Title VII of the Civil Rights Act "is consistent with either current or past employment."[13]

Employer

The EEOC regulations do not reiterate the statutory definition of employer which provides citations to the definitions used in other laws; rather, the final regulations provide a more concise definition drawn from the statutory references. Employer is defined as

> any person that employs an employee defined in §1635.2(c) of this part, and any agent of such person, except that, as limited by section 701(b)(1) and (2) of the Civil Rights Act of 1964 ..., an employer does not include an Indian tribe, or a bona fide private club (other than a labor organization) that is exempt from taxation under section 501(c) of the Internal Revenue Code of 1986.[14]

The definition does not specifically state that there is no individual liability for violations of GINA, as one commenter on the proposed regulations had suggested. The EEOC determined that it was not necessary to specifically include such a statement in the definition of employee.[15] In making this determination, the EEOC observed that GINA references the definition of employer used by Title VII of the Civil Right Act of 1964 and numerous courts have held that this definition does not allow for individual liability.[16]

Family Member

GINA's statutory definition of family member references ERISA Section 701(f)(2),[17] and also includes other individuals who are in first-, second-, third-, or fourth-degree relationships. The EEOC's final regulations provide that a family member with respect to an individual is "a person who is a dependent of that individual as a result of marriage, birth, adoption, or placement for adoption."[18] Although some commenters to the proposed regulations argued that dependents by adoption or placement by adoption should not be included since they did not share the same genetics as the adoptive parents, the EEOC rejected this argument, noting that Section 701(f)(2) of ERISA specifically referred to adoption, and that the acquisition of genetic information about an adoptive child could result in genetic discrimination.[19]

Family Medical History

Family medical history is not defined in the statute, but is used in the statutory prohibition on the acquisition of genetic information.[20] The EEOC final regulations define the term as meaning "information about the manifestation of disease or disorder in family members of the individual."[21]

Genetic Test

GINA's statutory language defines genetic test as "an analysis of human DNA, RNA, chromosomes, proteins, or metabolites, that detects genotypes, mutations, or chromosomal changes," but contains an exception for "an analysis of proteins or metabolites that does not detect genotypes, mutations, or chromosomal changes."[22] The EEOC's final regulations mirror the statutory language except that the regulations provide specific examples of genetic tests and of tests or procedures that are not genetic tests. For example, a genetic test includes a test to determine whether an individual has a BRCA1 or BRCA2 variant which would indicate a predisposition to breast cancer, and would include preimplantation genetic diagnosis on embryos.[23] One of the examples given in the regulations of a test that is not a genetic test is a test for cholesterol levels, since a cholesterol test does not detect mutations.[24] Similarly, testing for the presence of alcohol or illegal drugs is also not considered a genetic test since it is not an analysis of DNA or RNA, but a test to determine whether an individual has a genetic predisposition for alcoholism or drug use is a genetic test.[25]

Manifestation or Manifested

Since the statutory language of GINA refers to the manifestation of a disease,[26] the EEOC includes a definition of the term in final regulations. Manifestation or manifested is defined in the final regulations as meaning,

> with respect to a disease, disorder, or pathological condition, that an individual has been or could reasonably be diagnosed with the disease, disorder, or pathological condition by a health care professional with appropriate training and expertise in the field of medicine involved. For the purposes of this part, a disease, disorder, or pathological condition is not manifested if the diagnosis is based principally on genetic information.[27]

In its comments on this definition, the EEOC notes that when the diagnosis of a disease depends on both signs and symptoms and genetic information, the disease will be considered manifested.[28] It was emphasized, however, that such information is still subject to other laws, such as Title I of the ADA which regulates the acquisition and use of medical information.[29]

PROHIBITED PRACTICES IN GINA FINAL REGULATIONS

The EEOC final regulations echo the statutory language regarding prohibitions against discrimination. The statute and regulations provide that it is unlawful

- for an employer to discriminate against an individual on the basis of genetic information in regard to hiring, discharge, compensation, terms, conditions, or privileges of employment;[30]
- for an employment agency to fail or refuse to refer any individual for employment or otherwise discriminate against any individual because of genetic information of the individual;[31]
- for a labor organization to exclude or to expel from the membership of the organization, or otherwise discriminate against, any member because of genetic information;[32] and
- for any employer, labor organization, or joint labor-management committee controlling apprenticeship or other training programs to discriminate against an individual because of genetic information of the individual.[33]

The EEOC observes in its comments on the regulations that claims of harassment on the basis of genetic information may also be brought.[34]

The final regulations also reiterate the statutory language prohibiting actions that may limit, segregate, or classify employees because of genetic information.[35] A clarifying statement provides that a covered entity is not in violation of the prohibition on actions that limit, segregate, or classify employees due to genetic information if the action was required by a law or regulation mandating genetic monitoring.[36] The GINA regulations echo the statutory language prohibiting actions that cause a covered entity to discriminate,[37] but also include employers in this prohibition. The EEOC reasoned that although the GINA statutory language regarding employers does not include this prohibition, jurisprudence under Title VII of the Civil Rights Act includes employers' agents in the definition of employer. Thus, GINA would prohibit an employer from engaging in actions that would cause another covered entity acting as its agent to discriminate. To illustrate this, the EEOC gave an example of an employer who directed an employment agency to ask applicants for genetic information, thereby causing the employment agency, if they complied with the request, to be in violation of GINA.[38]

RETALIATION

GINA prohibits retaliation against an individual because the individual has opposed any act or practice that is unlawful under GINA or participated in an investigation, proceeding, or hearing concerning GINA.[39] The final regulations track this statutory language. In its comments, the EEOC notes that it believes the standard for retaliation under GINA was intended to be the same as that under Title VII as described in *Burlington Northern & Santa Fe Ry. v. White.*[40] In *Burlington*, the Supreme Court found that an anti-retaliation provision protects an individual if the action might have dissuaded a reasonable worker from making a discrimination claim.

ACQUISITION OF GENETIC INFORMATION

General Prohibitions

Providing nondiscrimination protections is a three-part process in GINA, as it is in the ADA. First, there is a general prohibition against discrimination;[41] second, there are prohibitions on the acquisition of information about the covered class that could result in discrimination; and third, there are confidentiality provisions.[42] GINA's statutory language left some ambiguity concerning when the "passive acquisition" of information was covered.[43] The EEOC resolved this issue by adding regulatory language defining "request" as including conducting an Internet search on an individual in such a way as is likely to result in obtaining genetic information; actively listening to third-party conversations; searching an individual's personal effects for the purpose of obtaining genetic information; and making requests for information about an individual's health status in a way that is likely to result in obtaining genetic information.[44]

Exceptions

The prohibition on the acquisition of information also contains exceptions, and the EEOC final regulations provide clarifying examples concerning these exceptions.

Inadvertent Requests or Acquisitions

The statutory language of GINA provides for an exception to the prohibition on the acquisition of information when a covered entity inadvertently requests or requires family medical history of the employee, individual, union member, or a family member.[45] The House Education and Labor Report noted that this exception "addresses the so-called 'water cooler' problem, in which an employer unwittingly receives otherwise protected genetic information in the form of family medical history through casual conversations with a worker."[46] The final regulations provide that if a covered entity inadvertently requests or requires genetic information relating to an individual or family member, the general prohibition does not apply. In its discussion of the final regulations, the EEOC notes that the statute only refers to family medical history, but states that it believes that "it is consistent with Congress's intent to extend the exception to any genetic information that an employer inadvertently acquires."[47]

When a covered entity requests medical information, the final regulations provide that, if a statement is provided warning individuals not to provide medical information, any information obtained is considered inadvertent. There would be no violation of GINA for obtaining information in this manner. However, even if a written notice is not provided, a covered entity may still be able to establish that information was obtained inadvertently.[48]

Wellness Programs

The second exception provided in GINA is for health or genetic services offered by the entity as part of a health or genetic services, including a wellness program.[49] To qualify for the exemption,

- the employee, individual, or union member must provide prior, knowing, voluntary, and written authorization;
- only the employee, individual, union member, or family member and the licensed health care profession or board certified genetic counselor involved in providing such services can receive individually identifiable information concerning the results of the services; and
- any individually identifiable genetic information is only available for such services and shall not be disclosed to the employer except in aggregate terms that do not identify individuals.[50]

The EEOC regulations reiterate the exception and its requirements.[51] In the proposed regulations, EEOC emphasized that such programs must be voluntary, and asked for comments concerning the appropriate level of inducement offered for participation in a wellness program. In the final regulations, the EEOC concluded that inducements may be offered to encourage individuals to participate in wellness programs, but inducements may not be offered to provide genetic information. The EEOC provides the following example in the regulations as a situation that does not violate GINA:

> A covered entity offers $150 to employees who complete a health risk assessment with 100 questions, the last 20 of them concerning family medical history and other genetic information. The instructions for completing the health risk assessment make clear that the inducement will be provided to all employees who respond to the first 80 questions, whether or not the remaining 20 questions concerning family medical history and other genetic information are answered.[52]

However, if the health risk assessment does not make clear which questions must be answered, it would violate GINA.[53]

Similarly, financial inducements may be offered to encourage participation in wellness programs for individuals who have voluntarily provided genetic information. In order to comply with GINA, these programs must also be offered to individuals with health conditions or life style choices that put them at an increased risk of developing a condition. For example, it would not violate GINA to offer $150 for participation in a weight loss program to employees who voluntarily disclose a family history of diabetes, heart disease, or high blood pressure, and to employees who have a current diagnosis of one of these conditions.[54]

The regulations also provide that they do not limit the rights or protections available under the ADA, other civil rights laws, or the Health Insurance Portability and Accountability Act (HIPAA). For example, an employer must make reasonable accommodations, as required under the ADA to enable a person with a disability to participate in a wellness program.[55]

Information Necessary for Certification Provisions

GINA provides an exception for information necessary for certification procedures under federal and state family and medical leave laws. This exception was described in the House report as "eliminat[ing] the potential for conflict with existing laws."[56] EEOC's final regulations track the statutory provision.[57]

Obtaining Genetic Information from Commercially and Publicly Available Sites

The fourth exception under GINA, like the first, concerns the inadvertent acquisition of genetic information by the purchase of documents, such as newspapers, that are commercially and publicly available and that include family medical history. This exception was intended to address the concern that GINA could be violated by such actions as the purchase of a newspaper "containing the obituary of an employee's parent who died of breast cancer."[58] The EEOC's regulations include electronic media, such as the Internet, television, and movies, as potential sources of genetic information.[59] In its discussion of this exception, the EEOC examines the factors used in deciding whether a document is commercially or publicly available and determines that the key criteria is "whether access requires permission of an individual or is limited to individuals in a particular group, not whether the source is categorized as a social networking site, personal Web site, or blog."[60] The EEOC also notes that the exception does not apply to genetic information gathered by actively searching for genetic information from commercially and publicly available sources, or to the acquisition of genetic information from a source likely to contain such information, such as a website that focuses on genetic testing.[61]

Genetic Monitoring of Biological Effects of Toxic Substances

The fifth exception applies when the information involved is to be used for genetic monitoring of the biological effects of toxic substances in the workplace. There are several conditions that must be met prior to applying this exception, including written notice of the monitoring, and knowing and voluntary authorization.[62] At the suggestion of several commenters to the proposed regulation, the EEOC added a provision to the final regulations stating that the covered entity may not retaliate or otherwise discriminate against an individual due to his or her refusal to participate in genetic monitoring that is not required by federal or state law.[63]

DNA Analysis for Law Enforcement Purposes

GINA contains a limited exception which allows employers and training programs that conduct DNA analysis for law enforcement purposes as a forensic laboratory or for purposes of human remains identification to request or require genetic information from their employees, but only when it is used for analysis of DNA identification markers for quality control to detect sample contamination. The EEOC in its comments to the final regulations notes that this exception is "very limited" and that "if the analysis is properly conducted, an employer or training program would not obtain health-related genetic information."[64]

Inquiries Made of Family Members

The EEOC final regulations provide that a covered entity does not violate GINA or the regulations when it requests or obtains information about a manifested disease of an employee whose family member is an employee for the same employer. The final regulations give the following example: "an employer will not violate this section by asking someone whose sister also works for the employer to take a post-offer medical examination that does not include requests for genetic information."[65]

Medical Examinations Relating to Employment

The prohibition on the acquisition of genetic information also applies to medical examinations relating to employment. The final regulations specifically provide that a covered entity must tell health care providers not to collect genetic information, including family history, during a medical examination relating to employment, and take appropriate action if it learns that genetic information is being collected. This action may include no longer using the services of a health care provider.[66]

The EEOC specifically declined to include an exemption that would permit a covered entity to request genetic information in order to evaluate whether an employee or applicant is able to safely and effectively perform the job. The EEOC's discussion of this section observes that the U.S. Customs and Immigration Services asked if there would be an exception allowing a covered entity to collect family medical history, such as a history of psychiatric disability, as part of determining whether to grant or deny a security clearance. The EEOC declined to provide such an exception, noting that there was no such exception in the statutory language or discussed in the legislative history.[67] The lack of a safety exemption may apply to situations such as that reportedly involving professional basketball player Eddy Curry. Mr. Curry was reportedly asked by the Chicago Bulls to take a genetic test to determine if he had hypertropic cardiomyopathy, a condition that can lead to sudden heart failure during exertion.[68] This is in contrast to the ADA as interpreted by the

Supreme Court in *Chevron v. Echazabal*,[69] where the Court found no violation of the ADA when an employer refused to hire an individual whose health would be endangered by the job. This issue may become more problematic as genetic information becomes more precise.

CONFIDENTIALITY

Generally, Title II of GINA requires that genetic information shall be maintained on separate forms and in separate medical files and be treated as a confidential medical record, and prohibits a covered entity from disclosing genetic information. These entities are considered to be in compliance with the maintenance of information requirements if the genetic information is treated as a confidential record under §102(d)(3)(B) of the Americans with Disabilities Act. However, the general prohibition on disclosure in GINA is subject to six exceptions, including disclosure to the employee.[70] GINA also contains a provision concerning the relationship of the confidentiality provisions with the HIPAA privacy rule. GINA does not prohibit an entity covered under HIPAA "from any use or disclosure of health information that is authorized for the covered entity under such regulations."[71]

The EEOC final regulations track the legislative language.[72] The EEOC in its discussion of the final regulations addresses several concerns raised by commenters. For example, the EEOC states that genetic information that had been placed in a personnel file prior to the effective date of GINA, need not be removed and its existence does not create a violation of GINA. However, disclosing such information to a third party would violate the law.[73]

ENFORCEMENT AND REMEDIES

Generally, GINA uses the remedies and enforcement mechanisms available in Title VII of the Civil Rights Act of 1964,[74] although for employees covered by the Government Employee Rights Act of 1991,[75] the Congressional Accountability Act of 1995,[76] chapter 5 of Title 3 of the U.S. Code,[77] or Section 717 of the Civil Rights Act of 1964,[78] the remedies and procedures track those acts and statutory provisions. The final regulations mirror the statutory provisions, and add a specific subsection referencing the remedies applicable to GINA. These include compensatory and punitive damages, reasonable attorneys' fees, and injunctive relief.[79]

CONSTRUCTION

Section 209 of GINA contains several rules of construction, including a provision concerning the relationship between Title I and Title II of the act.[80] GINA provides that nothing in Title II is to be construed to limit the rights or protections of an individual under any federal or state statute that provides equal or greater protection. In addition, nothing in Title II is to limit the rights or protections of an individual to bring an action, or provide for enforcement of, or penalties for, any violation under Title I of GINA, certain sections of ERISA, the Public Health Service Act, and the Internal Revenue Code. This provision has been referred to as a "firewall" between Titles I and II, and has been described as clarifying "that employers are not liable for health insurance violations under civil rights laws unless the employer has separately violated a provision of Title II governing employers."[81]

The final regulations mirror the statutory language and elaborate on the firewall provision. The regulations note that,

> [t]he firewall seeks to ensure that health plan or issuer provisions or actions are addressed and remedied through ERISA, the Public Health Service Act, or the Internal Revenue Code, while actions taken by employers and other GINA Title II covered entities are remedied through GINA Title II. Employers and other GINA Title II covered entities would remain liable for any of their actions that violate Title II, even where those actions involve access to health benefits, because such benefits are within the definition of compensation, terms, conditions, or privileges of employment. For example, an employer that fires an employee because of anticipated high health claims based on genetic information remains subject to liability under Title II.[82]

The EEOC's discussion of the final regulations also notes that over 30 states have laws concerning genetic discrimination. The EEOC states that it will provide information on these state and local laws on its website.[83]

Section 210 of GINA clarifies that the act does not cover medical information that is not genetic information about a manifested disease, disorder, or pathological condition, including a manifested disease, disorder, or pathological condition that has or may have a genetic basis.[84] The final regulations elaborate on the statutory language specifically stating that "the acquisition, use, and disclosure of medical information that is not genetic information about a manifested disease, disorder, or pathological condition is subject to applicable limitations under sections 103(d)(1)- (4) of the Americans with Disabilities Act (42 U.S.C. 12112(d)(1)-(4)), and regulations at 29 CFR 1630.13, 1630.14, and 1630.16."[85]

MEDICAL INFORMATION THAT IS NOT GENETIC INFORMATION

In its discussion of the final regulations, the EEOC notes that one commenter had expressed concern that individuals who have a manifested genetic disease that is not yet substantially limiting may not be covered under either law. The EEOC declined to address this issue, stating that it had no authority to expand the coverage of GINA. However, the EEOC observed that with the enactment of the ADA Amendments Act (ADAAA),[86] which expanded the definition of disability under the ADA, it is less likely that there would be a significant number of individuals who would not be covered by either act.[87]

End Notes

[1] 42 U.S.C. §2000ff et seq.

[2] For a discussion of the statutory provisions of GINA see CRS Report RL34584, The Genetic Information Nondiscrimination Act of 2008 (GINA), by Nancy Lee Jones and Amanda K. Sarata.

[3] GINA is a rarity among civil rights statutes since it does not address a long history of discrimination but rather attempts to ensure that new technologies do not give rise to discriminatory actions. For a discussion of the uniqueness of genetic information see CRS Report RL34376, Genetic Exceptionalism: Genetic Information and Public Policy, by Amanda K. Sarata.

[4] According to Peggy Mastroianni, EEOC's associate legal counsel, EEOC has received about 200 charges alleging GINA violations since the act took effect last year although EEOC has not yet issued a complaint under GINA. BNA's Health Care Daily, http://news.bna.com /hdln/HDLNWB/split_display.adp?fedfid=18392162&vname=hcenotallissues&wsn=49696 7000&fn=18392162&split=0. Prior to the enactment of GINA, the EEOC filed a complaint regarding genetic discrimination under the Americans with Disabilities Act (ADA), 42 U.S.C. §12101 et seq., which was ultimately settled. http://www.eeoc.gov/eeoc/newsroom/ release/2-9-01-c.cfm

[5] See CRS Report RL34376, Genetic Exceptionalism: Genetic Information and Public Policy, by Amanda K. Sarata.

[6] Interim final regulations have been issued under Title I. See 29 C.F.R. §2590.702, 74 FED. REG. 51683 (October 7, 2009). A discussion of Title I of GINA is beyond the scope of this report.
[7] 75 FED. REG. 68912 (November 9, 2010).
[8] 75 FED. REG. 68914 (November 9, 2010).
[9] *Id.*
[10] 29 C.F.R. §1635.2(c); 75 FED. REG. 68932 (November 9, 2010).
[11] See 75 FED. REG. 68914 (November 9, 2010).
[12] 519 U.S. 337 (1997).
[13] *Id.* at 342.
[14] 29 C.F.R. §1635.2(d); 75 FED. REG. 68932 (November 9, 2010).
[15] 75 FED. REG. 68914 (November 9, 2010).
[16] Id.
[17] 29 U.S.C. §1181(f)(2). This subsection provides that a person may become a dependent "through marriage, birth, or adoption or placement for adoption…."
[18] 29 C.F.R. § 1635.3(a); 75 FED. REG. 68933 (November 9, 2010).
[19] 75 FED. REG. 68915 (November 9, 2010).
[20] 42 U.S.C. §2000ff-1; 42 U.S.C. §2000ff-2; 42 U.S.C. §2000ff-3; 42 U.S.C. §2000ff-4.
[21] 29 C.F.R. § 1635.3(b); 75 FED. REG. 68933 (November 9, 2010).
[22] 42 U.S.C. §2000ff(7).
[23] 29 C.F.R. § 1635.3(f)(2); 75 FED. REG. 68933 (November 9, 2010).
[24] 29 C.F.R. § 1635.3(f)(3); 75 FED. REG. 68933 (November 9, 2010).
[25] 29 C.F.R. § 1635.3(f)(4); 75 FED. REG. 68933 (November 9, 2010).
[26] 42 U.S.C. §2000ff(4)(A)(iii); 42 U.S.C. §2000ff-9.
[27] 29 C.F.R. § 1635.3(g); 75 FED. REG. 68933-68934 (November 9, 2010).
[28] 75 FED. REG. 68917 (November 9, 2010).
[29] 42 U.S.C. §12112(d). For a general discussion of the ADA, including these provisions, see CRS Report 98-921, *The Americans with Disabilities Act (ADA): Statutory Language and Recent Issues*, by Nancy Lee Jones.
[30] 42 U.S.C. §2000ff-1; 29 C.F.R. §1635.4(a).
[31] 42 U.S.C. §2000ff-2; 29 C.F.R. §1635.4(b).
[32] 42 U.S.C. §2000ff-3; 29 C.F.R. §1635.4(c).
[33] 42 U.S.C. §2000ff-4; 29 C.F.R. §1635.4(d).
[34] 75 FED. REG. 68918 (November 9, 2010).
[35] 42 U.S.C. §2000ff-1; 42 U.S.C. §2000ff-2; 42 U.S.C. §2000ff-3; 42 U.S.C. §2000ff-4; 29 C.F.R. §1635.5, 75 FED. REG. 68934 (November 9, 2010).
[36] 29 C.F.R. §1635.5(a), 75 FED. REG. 68934 (November 9, 2010).
[37] 42 U.S.C. §2000ff-2; 42 U.S.C. §2000ff-3; 42 U.S.C. §2000ff-4; 29 C.F.R. §1635.6, 75 FED. REG. 68934 (November 9, 2010).
[38] 75 FED. REG. 68918 (November 9, 2010).
[39] 42 U.S.C. §2000ff-6(f).
[40] 548 U.S. 53 (2006). The EEOC discussion of this issue is at 75 FED. REG. 68918 (November 9, 2010).
[41] 42 U.S.C. §2000ff-1; 42 U.S.C. §2000ff-2; 42 U.S.C. §2000ff-3; 42 U.S.C. §2000ff-4; 29 C.F.R. §1635.4, 75 FED. REG. 68934 (November 9, 2010).
[42] 42 U.S.C. §2000ff-1; 42 U.S.C. §2000ff-2; 42 U.S.C. §2000ff-3; 42 U.S.C. §2000ff-4; 29 C.F.R. §1635.8, 75 FED. REG. 68934 (November 9, 2010).
[43] 75 FED. REG. 68919 (November 9, 2010).

[44] 29 C.F.R. §1635.8(a), 75 FED. REG. 68934 (November 9, 2010).

[45] 42 U.S.C. §2000ff-1; 42 U.S.C. §2000ff-2; 42 U.S.C. §2000ff-3; 42 U.S.C. §2000ff-4; 29 C.F.R. §1635.8(b)(1), 75 FED. REG. 68934 (November 9, 2010).

[46] H.Rept. 110-28, Part 1 at 37 (March 5, 2007).

[47] 75 FED. REG. 68919 (November 9, 2010).

[48] 29 C.F.R. §1635.8(b)(1)(i), 75 FED. REG. 68934 (November 9, 2010).

[49] For a discussion of the legal issues involving wellness programs generally, see CRS Report R40661, *Wellness Programs: Selected Legal Issues*, coordinated by Nancy Lee Jones.

[50] 42 U.S.C. §2000ff-1; 42 U.S.C. §2000ff-2; 42 U.S.C. §2000ff-3; 42 U.S.C. §2000ff-4.

[51] 29 C.F.R. §1635.8(b)(2), 75 FED. REG. 68935 (November 9, 2010).

[52] 29 C.F.R. §1635.8(b)(2)(ii)(A), 75 FED. REG. 68935 (November 9, 2010).

[53] 29 C.F.R. §1635.8(b)(2)(ii)(B), 75 FED. REG. 68935 (November 9, 2010).

[54] 29 C.F.R. §1635.8(b)(2)(iii), 75 FED. REG. 68935 (November 9, 2010).

[55] 29 C.F.R. §1635.8(b)(2)(iv), 75 FED. REG. 68936 (November 9, 2010).

[56] H.Rept. 110-28, Part 1 at 38 (March 5, 2007).

[57] 29 C.F.R. §1635.8(b)(3), 75 FED. REG. 68936 (November 9, 2010).

[58] H.Rept. 110-28, Part 1 at 38 (March 5, 2007).

[59] 29 C.F.R. §1635.8(b)(4), 75 FED. REG. 68936 (November 9, 2010).

[60] 75 FED. REG. 68925 (November 9, 2010).

[61] *Id.*

[62] 29 C.F.R. §1635.8(b)(5), 75 FED. REG. 68936 (November 9, 2010).

[63] *Id.*

[64] 75 FED. REG. 68926 (November 9, 2010).

[65] 29 C.F.R. §1635.8(c), 75 FED. REG. 68936 (November 9, 2010).

[66] 29 C.F.R. §1635.8(d), 75 FED. REG. 68937 (November 9, 2010).

[67] 75 FED. REG. 68926 (November 9, 2010).

[68] For a discussion of this situation and the use by Major League Baseball of genetic testing to determine the age of potential players see, Rhonda B. Evans, "'Striking Out': The Genetic Information Nondiscrimination Act of 2008 and Title II's Impact on Professional Sports Employers," 11 N. C. J. of Law and Technology 205 (Fall 2009) available at http://jolt.unc.edu/sites/default/files/Evans_Rhonda_v11i1_205_221.pdf. The application of GINA in this situation may turn on whether the condition is considered "manifested." See supra p. 4.

[69] 536 U.S. 73 (2002). But see UAW v. Johnson Controls, Inc., 499 U.S. 187 (1991), where the Court held that under the Civil Rights Act of 1964 employers could not enforce "fetal protection" policies that kept women, whether pregnant or with the potential to become pregnant, from jobs that might endanger a developing fetus. For a more detailed discussion of these cases see CRS Report RL31401, *The Americans with Disabilities Act: Supreme Court Decisions*, by Nancy Lee Jones.

[70] 42 U.S.C. §12112(d)(3)(B).

[71] *Id.*

[72] 29 C.F.R. §1635.9, 75 FED. REG. 68937 (November 9, 2010).

[73] 75 FED. REG. 68927 (November 9, 2010).

[74] 42 U.S.C. §2000e-4 et seq.

[75] 42 U.S.C. §2000e-16(b) and (c).

[76] 2 U.S.C. §1301 et seq.

[77] 3 U.S.C. §451-454.

[78] 42 U.S.C. § 2000e-16.

[79] 29 C.F.R. §1635.10(b), 75 FED. REG. 68937-68938 (November 9, 2010).
[80] 42 U.S.C. §2000ff-8.
[81] 154 Cong. Rec. H2972 (daily ed. May 1, 2008)(statement of Rep. Dingell).
[82] 29 C.F.R. §1635.11(b)(2), 75 FED. REG. 68938 (November 9, 2010).
[83] 75 FED. REG. 68929 (November 9, 2010).
[84] 42 U.S.C. §2000ff-9.
[85] 29 C.F.R. §1635.12, 75 FED. REG. 68939 (November 9, 2010).
[86] P.L. 110-325. For a discussion of the ADAAA see CRS Report RL34691, *The ADA Amendments Act: P.L. 110-325*, by Nancy Lee Jones.
[87] 75 FED. REG. 68931 (November 9, 2010).

In: Genetic Information, Health Laws ... ISBN: 978-1-61942-176-9
Editors: Gossling and Richards

Chapter 5

THE GENETIC INFORMATION NONDISCRIMINATION ACT OF 2008 (GINA)*

Amanda K. Sarata and Nancy Lee Jones

SUMMARY

On May 21, 2008, the Genetic Information Nondiscrimination Act of 2008 (GINA), referred to by its sponsors as the first civil rights act of the 21st century, was enacted. GINA, P.L. 110-233, prohibits discrimination based on genetic information by health insurers and employers. The sequencing of the human genome and subsequent advances raise hope for genetic therapies to cure disease, but this scientific accomplishment is not without potential problems. An employer or health insurer could decide to take adverse action based on a genetic predisposition to disease, and situations have arisen where discriminatory action based on genetic information did occur. In addition, there is evidence that the fear of genetic discrimination has an adverse effect on those seeking genetic testing, as well as on participation in genetic research. GINA was enacted to remedy this situation.

GINA is divided into two main parts: Title I, which prohibits discrimination based on genetic information by health insurers; and Title II, which prohibits discrimination in employment based on genetic information. Title I of GINA amends the Employee Retirement Income

* This is an edited, reformatted and augmented version of a Congressional Research Service publication, CRS Report for Congress RL34584, from www.crs.gov, dated June 13, 2011.

Security Act of 1974 (ERISA), the Public Health Service Act (PHSA), and the Internal Revenue Code (IRC), through the Health Insurance Portability and Accountability Act of 1996 (HIPAA), as well as the Social Security Act, to prohibit health insurers from engaging in genetic discrimination. Title II of GINA prohibits discrimination in employment because of genetic information and, with certain exceptions, prohibits an employer from requesting, requiring, or purchasing genetic information. The law prohibits the use of genetic information in employment decisions—including hiring, firing, job assignments, and promotions—by employers, unions, employment agencies, and labor-management training programs.

This report provides background on genetic information, legal implications regarding the use of this information, and relevant laws. It also discusses the statutory provisions of GINA and the regulations regarding both health insurance and employment.

INTRODUCTION

On May 21, 2008, the Genetic Information Nondiscrimination Act of 2008 (GINA), referred to by its sponsors as the first civil rights act of the 21st century, was enacted. GINA, P.L. 110-233, prohibits discrimination based on genetic information by health insurers and employers.

In April 2003, the sequence of the human genome was deposited into public databases. Scientists involved in the Human Genome Project (HGP)[1] reported that the finished sequence consists of overlapping fragments covering 99% of the coding regions of the human genome, with an accuracy of 99.999%.[2] These rapid advances provide powerful tools for determining the causes of, and potentially the cures for, many common, complex diseases such as diabetes, heart disease, Parkinson's disease, bipolar disorder, and asthma.

Although the sequence information should facilitate the identification of genes underlying disease and create a foundation for the development of genetic therapies, this scientific accomplishment is not without potential problems. For instance, the presence of a specific genetic variation may indicate a predisposition to disease but does not guarantee that the disease will manifest. An employer or health insurer could decide to take adverse action based on a genetic predisposition, and situations have arisen where discriminatory action based on genetic information did occur. GINA was enacted to remedy this potential situation. This report provides background on genetic information, legal implications regarding the use of this information, and relevant laws. It also discusses the statutory provisions of GINA, the

Department of Health and Human Service's (HHS's) regulations on health insurance, and the Equal Employment Opportunity Commission's (EEOC's) regulations on employment.[3]

BACKGROUND

Human Genome Research

In congressional testimony, Dr. Francis Collins, then Director of the National Human Genome Research Institute, described the potential that the information generated by the HGP holds for medicine and public health.4 He stated that

> the human genome sequence provides foundational information that now will allow development of a comprehensive catalog of all of the genome's components, determination of the function of all human genes, and deciphering of how genes and proteins work together in pathways and networks. Completion of the human genome sequence offers a unique opportunity to understand the role of genetic factors in health and disease, and to apply that understanding rapidly to prevention, diagnosis, and treatment. This opportunity will be realized through such genomics-based approaches as identification of genes and pathways and determining how they interact with environmental factors in health and disease, more precise prediction of disease susceptibility and drug response, early detection of illness, and development of entirely new therapeutic approaches.[5]

As Dr. Collins stated, with completion of the human genome sequence, scientists will now focus on understanding the clinical and public health implications of the sequence information. All disease has a genetic component and, therefore, genomic research has the potential to substantially reduce the collective burden of disease in the general population. Clinical genetic tests are becoming available at a rapid rate; in addition, private insurers are beginning to include some clinical genetic tests in their health insurance benefits packages as evidence of the tests' clinical validity accumulates.[6]

These scientific advances in genetics, while promising, are not without potential problems. The ethical, social, and legal implications of genetic research have been the subject of significant scrutiny and a portion of the funds for the Human Genome Project were set aside to support the analysis and research of these issues.[7]

Concerns about the Use of Genetic Information

As scientific knowledge about genetics becomes increasingly widespread, numerous researchers and commentators, including Dr. Francis Collins, have expressed concerns about how this information will be used.[8] In congressional testimony, Dr. Collins stated,

> while genetic information and genetic technology hold great promise for improving human heath, they can also be used in ways that are fundamentally unjust. Genetic information can be used as the basis for insidious discrimination....The misuse of genetic information has the potential to be a very serious problem, both in terms of people's access to employment and health insurance and the continued ability to undertake important genetic research.[9]

Legal cases of genetic discrimination have been few.[10] However, studies have shown that public fear of discrimination is substantial and negatively influences the uptake of genetic testing and the use of genetic information by consumers and health professionals. The Secretary's Advisory Committee on Genetics, Health and Society (SACGHS) learned that 68% of Americans are concerned about who would have access to their personal genetic information; 31% state this concern would prevent them from having a genetic test; and 68% agree that insurers would do everything possible to use genetic information to deny health coverage.[11] A 2010 survey found that Americans are increasingly concerned about access to their genetic information; specifically, this survey found that 71% of Americans are concerned about storage of and access to their information, with the same percentage concerned specifically about access by health insurers.[12]

In addition, SACGHS as well as its predecessor committee, the Secretary's Advisory Committee on Genetic Testing (SACGT), sponsored two public forums in 2000 and 2004 to gather perspectives on genetic discrimination. Many comments were received from patients, consumers, health professionals, scientists, genetic test developers, educators, industry representatives, policymakers, lawyers, students, and others representing a wide range of diverse ethnic and racial groups.[13] The comments and testimony revealed several anecdotal cases of discrimination. SACGT sent a letter to the Secretary of HHS urging support for nondiscrimination protections after the 2000 forum:

> During consultations with the public SACGT heard from many Americans who are concerned about the misuse of genetic information by

> third parties, such as health insurers and employers, and the potential for discrimination based on that information. Many stated that fear of genetic discrimination would dissuade them from undergoing a genetic test or participating in genetic research studies. Others stated that they would pay out of pocket for a genetic test to prevent the results from being placed in their medical record. Such concerns are a deterrent to advances in the field of genetic testing and may limit the realization of the benefits of genetic testing.[14]

A joint report by the Department of Labor, the Department of Health and Human Services, the Equal Employment Opportunity Commission (EEOC), and the Department of Justice summarized the various studies on discrimination based on genetic information and argued for the enactment of federal legislation. The report stated that "genetic predisposition or conditions can lead to workplace discrimination, even in cases where workers are healthy and unlikely to develop disease or where the genetic condition has no effect on the ability to perform work" and that "because an individual's genetic information has implications for his or her family members and future generations, misuse of genetic information could have intergenerational effects that are far broader than any individual incident of misuse."[15] Concluding that existing protections are minimal, the report went on to call for the enactment of legislation.

The National Council on Disability (NCD), an independent federal agency that advises the President and Congress on issues affecting individuals with disabilities, published a position paper on March 4, 2002, arguing for the enactment of federal legislation prohibiting genetic discrimination. The NCD argued that recent advances in genetic research have brought an increasing potential for genetic discrimination, that genetic discrimination is a historical and current reality, that genetic discrimination undermines the purposes of genetic research and testing, that genetic test information has little value for purposes of making employment decisions and insurance decisions, and that existing laws are insufficient to protect individuals from genetic discrimination.[16]

Title I of GINA extends the current HIPAA protections against discrimination by group health plans and issuers of health insurance in both the group and individual markets. HIPAA prohibits a group health plan or issuer of a group health plan from using genetic information to establish rules for eligibility or continued eligibility and provides that genetic information shall not be treated as a preexisting condition in the absence of the diagnosis of the condition related to such information. It also prohibits a group health plan or issuer of a group health plan from using genetic information in setting a premium contribution.

Federal Law Relating to Genetic Discrimination Prior to GINA

Health Insurance Portability and Accountability Act of 1996 (HIPAA)

These protections apply to individuals within the group plans; however, they do not apply to the acceptance of the whole group or to the premiums set for the group. Thus, HIPAA prohibits group health plans or issuers of group health plans from charging an individual a higher premium than a similarly situated individual; however, the law does not prevent an entire group from being charged more. The HIPAA nondiscrimination provisions do not apply to individual health insurance policies, and genetic information may be used to set premiums for individual policies (although HIPAA establishes both guaranteed issue for individuals who lose group coverage and guaranteed renewal for those with existing individual coverage).

HIPAA would not prohibit group health plans or issuers of plans (i.e., insurers) from requiring or requesting genetic information or testing and does not prevent them from excluding coverage for a particular condition or imposing lifetime caps on all benefits, or on specific benefits. Finally, HIPAA does not address the use of genetic information in contexts other than health insurance, such as employment.

Under the HIPAA Privacy Rule, health plans and insurers may use or disclose health information for payment and other health care operations, including underwriting, premium rating, and other activities related to the creation, renewal, or replacement of an insurance contract.

Americans with Disabilities Act

The Americans with Disabilities Act (ADA)[17] prohibits discrimination against an individual with a disability in employment, public services, public accommodations, and communications. The threshold issue in any ADA case is whether the individual alleging discrimination is an individual with a disability. The ADA as amended by the ADA Amendments Act, P.L. 110-325, defines the term disability with respect to an individual as having "(A) a physical or mental impairment that substantially limits one or more of the major life activities of such individual; (B) a record of such an impairment; or (C) being regarded as having such an impairment (as described in paragraph

(3)).”[18] Although the statutory language of the ADA does not reference genetic traits, there was a discussion of the issue during congressional debate of the original legislation.[19] So far there have been no judicial decisions specifically dealing with genetic predisposition to disease and the ADA, but one case was brought by the EEOC and settled.[20] In addition, Terri Seargent filed with the EEOC alleging genetic discrimination and received a determination on November 21, 2000, that the EEOC’s investigation supported her allegation of discrimination under the ADA.[21]

The ADA had been interpreted by the EEOC, prior to the enactment of the ADA Amendments Act, as including genetic information relating to illness, disease, or other disorders.[22] The legislative history was cited by the EEOC in its guidance to the definition of disability for its compliance manual. In this guidance, the EEOC examined the definition of disability under the ADA, noting that the definition was composed of three prongs: disability means (1) a physical or mental impairment that substantially limits one or more of the major life activities of an individual, (2) a record of such an impairment, or (3) being regarded as having such an impairment.[23] It was under the third prong that the EEOC determined that discrimination based on genetic information relating to illness, disease, or other disorders was prohibited.

Although this EEOC interpretation was widely heralded as a significant step for the protection of rights for individuals whose genes indicate an increased susceptibility to illness, disease, or other disorders, it is limited in its application and was even more limited by Supreme Court decisions on the definition of disability.[24] However, the EEOC has not withdrawn this guidance, and at Senate hearings EEOC Commissioner Paul Miller stated that the ADA “can be interpreted to prohibit employment discrimination based on genetic information. However, the ADA does not explicitly address the issue and its protections are limited and uncertain.” In addition, Commissioner Miller observed that even if the ADA were found to cover genetic discrimination, the requirements of the ADA may not protect workers from all types of genetic discrimination. He stated, “for example, the ADA does not protect workers from requirements or requests to provide genetic information to their employers.... In addition, once the applicant is hired, the employer may request that the employee take a medical exam, such as a genetic test, if the employer can demonstrate that the information from that test is job related and consistent with business necessity.”[25]

Although the combination of the ADA’s legislative history and the EEOC’s guidance led some commentators to argue that the ADA would cover genetic discrimination, the merit of these arguments has been uncertain since there have been no reported cases holding that the ADA prohibits genetic discrimination. This uncertainty increased after Supreme Court decisions on the definition of disability under the ADA, although the Supreme Court's decisions did not directly address ADA coverage of genetic discrimination.[26]

The ADA Amendments Act rejected the Supreme Court's limited interpretation of the definition of disability, and amended the ADA to provide for broader coverage. However, the ADA Amendments Act does not specifically mention genetic discrimination although the expanded definition would increase the likelihood of coverage. Even if the ADA was found to cover genetic discrimination, GINA's protections are more targeted to protecting genetic information.

Executive Order

On February 8, 2000, President Clinton issued an executive order prohibiting discrimination against federal employees based on protected genetic information. The executive order defines "protected genetic information" as "(A) information about an individual's genetic tests; (B) information about the genetic tests of an individual's family members; or (C) information about the occurrence of a disease; or medical condition or disorder in family members of the individual." Current health status information would not be protected under this executive order unless it was derived from the information described above. The EEOC has issued guidance on the executive order.[27]

State Statutes Relating to Genetic Nondiscrimination

Many states have enacted statutes dealing with various aspects of genetic discrimination. Early state statutes focused on particular genetic conditions. The first statute to prohibit discrimination based on a genetic trait was enacted in North Carolina and prohibited employment discrimination based on the sickle cell trait. In 1991 Wisconsin became the first state to enact a comprehensive law to prohibit discrimination based on genetic test results. Currently, the states vary in their provisions with some prohibiting discrimination in employment while others deal solely with discrimination in insurance. In its discussion of the final regulations, the EEOC notes that over 30 states have laws concerning genetic discrimination. The EEOC states that it will provide information on these state and local laws on its website.[28]

In a 2008 survey of state law, the National Conference of State Legislatures similarly found that 34 states and the District of Columbia have enacted genetic nondiscrimination in employment laws.[29] These laws vary and the NCSL noted the following:

> All laws prohibit discrimination based on the results of genetic tests; many extend the protections to inherited characteristics, and some include test results of family members, family history and information about genetic testing, such as the receipt of genetic services. Most states also restrict employer access to genetic information, with some prohibiting employers from requesting, requiring and obtaining genetic information or genetic test results, or directly or indirectly performing or administering genetic tests. Some states may also make exceptions to statutory requirements if, for example, genetic information may identify individuals who may be a safety risk in the workplace.[30]

A related survey found that 47 states and the District of Columbia have passed laws pertaining to the use of genetic information in health insurance.[31] Many state genetic laws also include specific provisions relating to genetic privacy.[32] In a 2008 survey, 27 states were found to require consent to disclose genetic information while 17 states require informed consent for a third party to perform or require a genetic test or obtain genetic information. Nineteen states were found that establish specific penalties for violating genetic privacy laws.[33]

Although these state statutes do provide some measure of protection against discrimination, they do not cover employer self-funded plans providing private health insurance for employees and their dependents. These plans are exempt from state insurance laws due to the preemption provision in the federal Employee Retirement Income Security Act (ERISA).[34] Since 55% of covered workers obtain their coverage through self-funded plans, the ERISA exemption limits the application of state laws significantly.[35]

On May 21, 2008, GINA was signed into law. The path to enactment of P.L. 110-233 was lengthy and tortuous. H.R. 493, the Genetic Information Nondiscrimination Act of 2007, was introduced by Representative Slaughter with 143 cosponsors on January 16, 2007. After being reported out of the House Education and Labor Committee, the House Energy and Commerce Committee, and the House Ways and Means Committee, the bill passed the House on April 25, 2007, by a vote of 420 to 3.

Genetic Information Nondiscrimination Act of 2008 (GINA)

Background

On April 24, 2008, the Senate took up H.R. 493, replaced the existing language with an amendment in the nature of a substitute, added new language strengthening the "firewall" between Title I (discrimination by health insurers) and Title II (discrimination in employment), and passed the measure, as amended, by a vote of 95-0. The House passed H.R. 493 (as amended) on May 1, 2008. On May 2, 2008, both the House and Senate passed H.Con.Res. 340 to make corrections in the enrollment of H.R. 493. These changes would

- revise deadlines for implementation of requirements related to Medicare supplemental policies;
- exempt an employer that conducts DNA analysis for purposes of human remains identification from the prohibition against an employer, labor organization, or joint labor-management committee requesting, requiring, or purchasing an employee's genetic information; and
- remove the requirement that DNA analysis conducted by an employer for law enforcement purposes as a forensics laboratory be included in the Combined DNA Index System.

The first legislation relating to genetic discrimination was introduced in 1995 by Representative Slaughter (H.R. 2748, 104th Cong.) and Representative Stearns (H.R. 2690, 104th Cong.). In each subsequent Congress legislation was introduced, and twice legislation passed the Senate. In the 108th Congress, the Senate passed the Genetic Information Nondiscrimination Act of 2003 (S. 1053).[36] This bill would have prohibited health insurance plans from denying enrollment or charging higher premiums to individuals based on the individual's or family members' genetic information. In addition, the bill banned the collection, use, and disclosure of genetic information for insurance underwriting purposes. In the employment context, this bill would have prohibited the use of genetic information in employment decisions, such as hiring, firing, job assignments, and promotions. The bill also would have prevented the acquisition and disclosure of genetic information as well as applied the procedures and remedies authorized under the Civil Rights Act of

1964 to cases of genetic discrimination. Although President Bush supported genetic discrimination legislation and the House held a hearing in July 2004,[37] the House did not pass a bill in the 108th Congress.

In the 109th Congress, S. 306, the Genetic Information Nondiscrimination Act of 2005, was introduced by Senator Snowe on February 7, 2005. The Senate Health, Education, Labor and Pensions Committee reported S. 306 out with an amendment in the nature of a substitute by a voice vote. The bill was passed, with an amendment, on February 17, 2005, by a vote of 98-0.

The amendment would have deleted former Section 103 which would have added a prohibition of discrimination based on genetic information or services in church health insurance plans to the Internal Revenue Code because this provision had to originate in the House. A companion bill, H.R. 1227, was introduced in the House on March 10, 2005, by Representative Biggert but did not pass.

Overview of Statutory Provisions

GINA contains a statement of findings which discusses the significance of the sequencing of the human genome, the history of discrimination based on genetics, and the inadequacy of current federal and state laws. The statute is then divided into three titles: Title I, which prohibits genetic discrimination in health insurance, Title II, which prohibits genetic discrimination in employment, and Title III, which contains miscellaneous provisions on severability and child labor protections.

Definition of Genetic Information

One of the most discussed provisions of GINA was the definition of genetic information. Discussions were focused on decisions that would impact the term's scope, centering largely on the exclusions for the definition (i.e., basic demographic information that implies genetic information, such as sex) as well as how to incorporate the concept of family history. Specifically, the definition of genetic information relies on three terms, two defined in the law—"genetic test" and "family member"—and one added through regulation, "manifestation" or "manifested." Together, these terms serve to delineate the scope of the law's protections.

Both Title I and Title II contain a definition of genetic information which states the following (key terms are in bold, emphasis added):

> GENETIC INFORMATION-(A) IN GENERAL -The term 'genetic information' means, with respect to any individual, information about—(i) such individual's genetic tests, (ii) the genetic tests of family members of such individual, and (iii) the manifestation of a disease or disorder in family members of such individual.(B) INCLUSION OF GENETIC SERVICES AND PARTICIPATION IN GENETIC RESEARCH -Such term includes, with respect to any individual, any request for, or receipt of, genetic services, or participation in clinical research which includes genetic services, by such individual or any family member of such individual. (C) EXCLUSIONS -The term 'genetic information' shall not include information about the sex or age of any individual.[38]

As mentioned previously, regulations have been promulgated implementing both Titles of GINA. The Departments of Health and Human Services, Treasury, and Labor jointly issued interim final regulations with request for comments implementing Sections 101 through 103 of Title I of GINA[39], excluding §104 ("Amendments to title XVIII of the Social Security Act relating to medigap") and §105 ("Privacy and confidentiality"). The Department of Health and Human Services, Office for Civil Rights, issued a proposed rule to implement §105,[40] and §104 incorporates, by reference to the Social Security Act, Section 1882, provisions of a model NAIC regulation which addresses Medigap issuers.[41] Additionally, the Equal Employment Opportunity Commission (EEOC) has issued regulations for Title II of GINA.

All of these regulations follow the statutory definition for "genetic information." The EEOC regulations clarify that neither race nor ethnicity (if this information is not derived from genetic tests) are considered to be genetic information.[42]

Definition of Genetic Test

As is the case with the definition for the term genetic information, the definition of genetic test is also of pivotal importance to defining the scope, and ultimately determining the impact, of the nondiscrimination protections in GINA. Importantly, this definition is different in Title I and Title II of the act. The Title I definition exempts genetic tests that are "an analysis of proteins or metabolites that [are] *directly related to a manifested disease, disorder, or pathological condition* that could reasonably be detected by a health care professional with appropriate training and expertise in the field of medicine involved." Title II defines genetic test as

a) IN GENERAL.—The term "genetic test" means an analysis of human DNA, RNA, chromosomes, proteins, or metabolites, that detects genotypes, mutations, or chromosomal changes.
b) Exceptions.—The term "genetic test" does not mean an analysis of proteins or metabolites that does not detect genotypes, mutations, or chromosomal changes.[43]

While Title II does not include the exception regarding manifested diseases contained in Title I, it does contain Section 210, which states,

> An employer, employment agency, labor organization, or joint labor-management committee shall not be considered to be in violation of this title based on the use, acquisition, or disclosure of medical information that is not genetic information about a manifested disease, disorder, or pathological condition of an employee or member, including a manifested disease, disorder, or pathological condition that has or may have a genetic basis.[44]

The interim final regulations follow the statutory language with respect to the definition of genetic test except that they provide specific examples of genetic and non-genetic tests to illustrate the definition's scope.

The EEOC's final regulations also mirror the statutory language except that the regulations provide specific examples of genetic tests and of tests or procedures that are not genetic tests. For example, a genetic test includes a test to determine whether an individual has a BRCA1 or BRCA2 variant which would indicate a predisposition to breast cancer, and would include preimplantation genetic diagnosis on embryos.[45] One of the examples given in the regulations of a test that is not a genetic test is a test for cholesterol levels, since a cholesterol test does not detect mutations. Similarly, testing for the presence of alcohol or illegal drugs is also not considered a genetic test since it is not an analysis of DNA or RNA, but a test to determine whether an individual has a genetic predisposition for alcoholism or drug use is a genetic test.[46]

Genetic Nondiscrimination and Health Insurance

Overview of Health Insurance Provisions

Title I of GINA strengthens and clarifies existing HIPAA nondiscrimination and portability provisions through amendments to the Employee Retirement Income Security Act of 1974 (ERISA), the Public Health Service Act (PHSA), and the Internal Revenue Code (IRC), as well as to the Social Security Act (SSA). In this way, group plans under ERISA, group and individual plans under the PHSA, Church Plans under the IRC, and Medigap plans under the SSA are all brought under the jurisdiction of the law. The complexity of the health care financing system required this approach to extend protection to all covered individuals, regardless of their insurance situation. The HHS interim final regulations implement Sections 101, 102, and 103 of Title I of GINA; as mentioned above, they do not address the application of GINA to Medigap issuers nor do they implement §105 of the title.[47]

Prohibited Health Insurer Practices

Broadly, GINA prohibits health insurers from engaging in three practices: (1) using genetic information about an individual to adjust a group plan's premiums, or, in the case of individual plans, to deny coverage, adjust premiums, or impose a preexisting condition exclusion; (2) requiring or requesting genetic testing; and (3) requesting, requiring, or purchasing genetic information for underwriting purposes. Each of these provisions is discussed below in more detail, and where applicable, modifications made by the regulations are noted.

Discrimination in Premium Setting and Eligibility Prohibited

GINA prohibits health plans, group and individual health insurers and issuers, and issuers of Medicare supplemental policies from adjusting a group or individual's premium based on genetic information about an individual in the group, an individual seeking individual coverage, or an individual's family members. It also prohibits individual insurers from conditioning eligibility or continuing eligibility on genetic information, and prohibits individual insurers from treating genetic information as a preexisting condition. Issuers of supplemental Medicare policies may not deny or condition the issuance of a policy based on genetic information (and may not impose a preexisting condition exclusion based on genetic information).

Genetic Testing Requests or Requirements Prohibited

GINA prohibits health plans, group and individual health insurers and issuers, and issuers of Medicare supplemental policies from requesting or requiring that individuals or their family members undergo a genetic test. This prohibition does not limit the authority of a health care professional to request that an individual undergo genetic testing as part of his or her course of health care. The act provides for a research exception to this provision, by allowing a group or individual insurance issuer to request, but not require, an individual to undergo genetic testing if specific conditions are met.

Collection and Use of Genetic Information Restricted

GINA prohibits health plans, group and individual health insurers and issuers, and issuers of Medicare supplemental policies from requesting, requiring, or purchasing genetic information for the purposes of underwriting prior to an individual's enrollment or in connection with enrollment. "Incidental collection" of genetic information would not be considered a violation. The HHS final interim rules clarify that "purposes of underwriting" does not include a request for family history or other genetic information to make a determination whether a benefit is medically appropriate for purposes of payment.[48]

Application to Genetic Information of a Fetus or Embryo

Title I of the act clarifies that genetic discrimination based on the genetic information of either the fetus of a pregnant woman or an embryo legally held by an individual or family member is prohibited. The HHS interim final regulations do not modify this provision.[49]

Rule of Construction

GINA provides clearly that nothing in the act should be construed to preclude the use of information about a manifested disease or disorder in an individual (or an individual's family member) by health plans, group and individual health insurers and issuers, and issuers of Medicare supplemental policies to establish premiums or conditions of eligibility. The HHS interim final regulations additionally clarify that insurers may not utilize the manifestation of a disease in an individual in a group as genetic information about other group members in determining the premium (for example, in the case of family members covered under the same policy, where the manifestation of a disease or condition in an individual might be relevant to the other family members' risk of manifesting that same disease or condition).[50] In addition, nothing in the act should be construed to prohibit health plans, group and individual health insurers and issuers, and issuers of Medicare supplemental policies from obtaining or using the results of genetic tests to determine payment. However, only the minimum amount of information required to achieve this purpose may be requested. HHS's interim final regulations clarify that where the appropriateness of a treatment depends on the patient's genetic makeup, an insurer may condition payment on the results of a genetic test or may deny payment for the treatment in the absence of the genetic test.[51] A double mastectomy, for example, might be indicated for an individual without a personal history of breast cancer only in the presence of a positive BRCA1/2 genetic test result; an insurer might not cover the surgical procedure only in the presence of family history of disease but in the absence of a confirmatory genetic test. However, the rules explain that in a case like this, the use of the genetic information to determine payment would not be a violation of GINA.

Privacy and Confidentiality

GINA directs the Secretary of Health and Human Services to revise the HIPAA Privacy Rule[52] to reflect that genetic information shall be treated as health information and the use or disclosure by a covered entity of protected health information (i.e., genetic information) for the purposes of underwriting shall not be a permitted use or disclosure. The Secretary, in consultation with the Secretaries of Labor and the Treasury, had 12 months after enactment of the act to issue final regulations to carry out these revisions. On October 7, 2009, the Department of Health and Human Services, Office for Civil Rights, published a proposed rule to implement this section. Among other things, the proposed rule would provide that

> Notwithstanding any other provision of this subpart [the HIPAA Privacy Rule], a health plan shall not use or disclose protected health information that is genetic information for underwriting purposes.[53]

Additionally, under the terms of the proposed rule, the use of an individual's genetic information for underwriting purposes is barred even if authorized by an individual.[54]

Remedies and Enforcement

GINA permits the Secretary to impose a penalty of $100 per day per beneficiary or participant to whom the failure relates during a period of noncompliance with the provisions in Title I. Where willful neglect was found, there is established a minimum penalty of $2,500, or $15,000 for more severe or prolonged violations. There are three limitations to the penalties that may be imposed by the Secretary. First, the penalty does not apply if the person otherwise liable for the penalty did not know that the noncompliance occurred. Second, the penalty does not apply to failures corrected within 30 days (in cases not due to willful neglect). Finally, a limit to the total penalty for unintentional failures is set at $500,000 or 10% of the aggregate amount paid or incurred by the plan sponsor during the preceding year for group health plans. The HHS interim final regulations are silent on the HHS and DOL secretarial enforcement authorities regarding the use of genetic information that were added under GINA; these will be addressed in future rulemaking.[55]

Genetic Nondiscrimination and Employment

Overview of Employment Provisions

GINA prohibits discrimination in employment because of genetic information and, with certain exceptions, prohibits an employer from requesting, requiring, or purchasing genetic information. The law prohibits the use of genetic information in employment decisions, including hiring; firing; job assignments; and promotions by employers, unions, employment agencies, and labor-management training programs. The EEOC has issued regulations for Title II which generally closely track the statutory language.[56]

Definition of Employee and Employer

GINA defines employees and employers as those defined in Section 701(b) and (f) of Title VII of the Civil Rights Act of 1964,[57] a state employee or employer as defined in Section 304(a) of the Government Employee Rights Act of 1991,[58] and a covered employee or employing office as defined in Section 101 of the Congressional Accountability Act.[59] Generally, this includes employees and applicants working in the private sector for an employer who employs 15 or more employees, federal and state governments, as well as congressional employees. The corresponding employers of these individuals, as well as employment agencies, labor organizations, and training programs, also are covered by the law. The EEOC's regulations echo the statutory language regarding employees and also include former employees.[60]

Prohibited Employment Practices

As noted previously, GINA prohibits the use of genetic information in employment decisions, including hiring, firing, job assignments, and promotions by employers, unions, employment agencies, and labor-management training programs.[61] In addition, an employer, employment agency, labor union, or training program may not "request, require or purchase genetic information" with respect to the employee, individual, union member, or family member.[62]

Exceptions to Prohibited Practices

There are statutory exceptions to the prohibition on the acquisition of genetic information for employers, employment agencies, labor unions, and training programs.[63] However, GINA provides that, even if an exception applies, genetic information may not be used in a manner that violates nondiscrimination or confidentiality requirements.[64]

Inadvertent Requests

The first exception applies when one of these entities inadvertently requests or requires family medical history of the employee, individual, union member, or a family member. The House Education and Labor Report noted that this exception "addresses the so-called 'water cooler' problem, in which an employer unwittingly receives otherwise protected genetic information in the form of family medical history through casual conversations with a worker."[65] Family medical history is not defined in the statute but the EEOC regulations define the term as meaning "information about the manifestation of disease or disorder in family members of the individual."[66]

Wellness Programs

The second exception is for health or genetic services offered by the entity as part of a wellness program.[67] To qualify for the exemption:

- the employee, individual or union member must provide prior, knowing, voluntary, and written authorization;
- only the employee, individual, union member, or family member and the licensed health care profession or board certified genetic counselor involved in providing such services can receive individually identifiable information concerning the results of the services; and

- any individually identifiable genetic information is only available for such services and shall not be disclosed to the employer except in aggregate terms that do not identify individuals.

The EEOC regulations reiterate the exception and its requirements[68] but also provide that inducements may be offered to encourage individuals to participate in wellness programs. However, these inducements may not be offered to provide genetic information. The EEOC provides the following example in the regulations as a situation that does not violate GINA:

> A covered entity offers $150 to employees who complete a health risk assessment with 100 questions, the last 20 of them concerning family medical history and other genetic information. The instructions for completing the health risk assessment make clear that the inducement will be provided to all employees who respond to the first 80 questions, whether or not the remaining 20 questions concerning family medical history and other genetic information are answered.[69]

In contrast, if the health risk assessment does not make clear which questions must be answered, it would violate GINA.[70]

The regulations also provide that they do not limit the rights or protections available under the ADA, other civil rights laws, or the Health Insurance Portability and Accountability Act (HIPAA). For example, an employer must make reasonable accommodations, as required under the ADA to enable a person with a disability to participate in a wellness program.

Certification Procedures under Medical Leave Laws

The third statutory exception is for information necessary for certification procedures under federal and state family and medical leave laws. This exception was described as "eliminat[ing] the potential for conflict with existing laws."[71] The EEOC regulations track the statutory provisions.[72]

Inadvertent Acquisition of Genetic Information by Purchase of Documents

The fourth exception, like the first, concerns the inadvertent acquisition of genetic information by the purchase of documents, such as newspapers, that are commercially and publicly available and that include family medical history. This exception was intended to address the concern that GINA could be violated by such actions as the purchase of a newspaper "containing the obituary of an employee's parent who died of breast cancer."[73] The EEOC's regulations include electronic media, such as the Internet, television, and movies, as potential sources of genetic information.[74] In its discussion of this exception, the EEOC examines the factors used in deciding whether a document is commercially or publicly available and determines that the key criterion is "whether access requires permission of an individual or is limited to individuals in a particular group, not whether the source is categorized as a social networking site, personal Web site, or blog."[75] The EEOC also notes that the exception does not apply to genetic information gathered by actively searching for genetic information from commercially and publicly available sources, or to the acquisition of genetic information from a source likely to contain such information, such as a website that focuses on genetic testing.[76]

Genetic Monitoring of Toxic Substances

The fifth exception applies when the information involved is to be used for genetic monitoring of the biological effects of toxic substances in the workplace. However, in order for this exception to apply,

- the employer, employment agency, labor union, or training program must provide written notice of the genetic monitoring to the employee;
- the employee, individual, or union member must provide prior, knowing, voluntary, and written authorization; or the genetic monitoring is required by federal or state law;
- the employee, individual, or union member must be informed of individual monitoring results;
- the monitoring must be in compliance with federal genetic monitoring regulations, or state genetic monitoring regulations; and
- the employer, employment agency, labor union, or training program, excluding any licensed health care professional or board certified genetic counselor, must receive the results only in aggregate terms that do not disclose the identity of specific employees.

DNA Analysis for Law Enforcement Purposes

There is a sixth exception for employers and training programs but not for employment agencies or labor unions. This exception, which was changed by H.Con.Res. 340, would allow employers and training programs that conduct DNA analysis for law enforcement purposes as a forensic laboratory or for purposes of human remains identification to request or require genetic information from their employees, but only when it is used for analysis of DNA identification markers for quality control to detect sample contamination. The EEOC notes that this is a very limited exception.[77]

Confidentiality of Genetic Information

Generally, GINA requires that genetic information shall be maintained on separate forms and in separate medical files and be treated as a confidential medical record, and prohibits employers, employment agencies, labor unions, and joint labor-management committees from disclosing genetic information. These entities are considered to be in compliance with the maintenance of information requirements if the genetic information is treated as a confidential record under § 102(d)(3)(B) of the Americans with Disabilities Act.[78] However, the general prohibition on disclosure is subject to six exceptions. Genetic information may be disclosed

- to the employee or member of a labor union (or family member receiving genetic services) at the written request of the employee or member;
- to an occupational or other health researcher if the research is conducted in compliance with 45 C.F. R. Part 46, which provides for protection of human research subjects;
- in response to a court order except that only the genetic information expressly authorized by the order shall be disclosed; if the court order was obtained without the knowledge of the employee or member to whom the information refers, the employee or member shall be informed of the court order and the information may be disclosed;
- to government officials who are investigating compliance with Title II of GINA, if the information is relevant;
- where such disclosure is made in connection with the certification provisions of the Family and Medical Leave Act or state family and medical leave laws; or
- to a federal, state, or local public health agency regarding a contagious disease that presents an imminent hazard of death or life-threatening illness, and there is notification.

GINA also contains a provision concerning the relationship of the confidentiality provisions with the HIPAA Privacy Rule. GINA does not prohibit an entity covered under HIPAA "from any use or disclosure of health information that is authorized for the covered entity under such regulations."

The EEOC final regulations track the legislative language.[79] The EEOC in its discussion of the final regulations addresses several concerns raised by commenters. For example, the EEOC states that genetic information that had been placed in a personnel file prior to the effective date of GINA, need not be removed and its existence does not create a violation of GINA. However, disclosing such information to a third party would violate the law.[80]

Remedies and Enforcement

Generally, GINA uses the remedies and enforcement mechanisms available in Title VII of the Civil Rights Act of 1964,[81] although for employees covered by the Government Employee Rights Act of 1991, the Congressional Accountability Act of 1995, chapter 5 of Title 3 of the U.S. Code, or Section 717 of the Civil Rights Act of 1964, the remedies and procedures track those acts and statutory provisions. The EEOC regulations describe these remedies as compensatory and punitive damages, reasonable attorney's fees, including expert fees, and injunctive relief, including reinstatement and hiring, back pay, and other equitable remedies.[82]

Disparate Impact

Section 703(k) of Title VII of the Civil Rights Act of 1964 provides for a cause of action based on the disparate impact of a particular employment practice on employment based on race, color, religion, sex, or national origin.[83] GINA specifically provides that such disparate impact does not create a cause of action under its provisions. However, GINA requires that a commission be established six years after the date of enactment to review the science of genetics and make recommendations to Congress regarding whether to provide a disparate impact cause of action under GINA.

Construction

Section 209 of GINA contains several rules of construction, including a provision concerning the relationship between Title I and Title II of the act. GINA provides that nothing in Title II is to be construed to limit the rights or protections of an individual under any federal or state statute that provides equal or greater protection. In addition, nothing in Title II is to limit the rights or protections of an individual to bring an action, or provide for enforcement of, or penalties for, any violation under Title I of GINA, certain sections of ERISA, the Public Health Service Act, and the Internal Revenue Code. This provision has been referred to as a "firewall" between Titles I and II, and has been described as clarifying "that employers are not liable for health insurance violations under civil rights laws unless the employer has separately violated a provision of Title II governing employers."[84]

GINA also states that it does not

- apply to the Armed Forces repository of specimen samples for the identification of remains;
- limit or expand the protections, rights, or obligations of employees or employers under applicable workers' compensation laws;
- limit the authority of a federal department or agency to conduct or sponsor health research conducted in compliance with rules for research on human subjects;
- limit the statutory or regulatory authority of the Occupational Safety and Health Administration or the Mine Safety and Health Administration regarding workplace safety and health laws and regulations; or
- require any specific benefit for an employee or member or a family member under any group health plan.

Section 209 also specifies that any reference in Title II to genetic information concerning an individual or family member also includes the genetic information of any fetus carried by a pregnant woman. In addition, genetic information on any embryo legally held by the individual or family member would also be included in the reference to genetic information.

Finally, Section 209 provides that Title II does not prohibit the activity of a group health plan or health insurance issuer offering group health insurance coverage that is authorized by Title I, and certain sections of ERISA, the Public Health Service Act, and the Internal Revenue Code.

Manifested Diseases

Section 210 of GINA clarifies that the act does not cover medical information that is not genetic information about a manifested disease, disorder, or pathological condition, including a manifested disease, disorder, or pathological condition that has or may have a genetic basis. The final EEOC regulations elaborate on the statutory language specifically stating that "the acquisition, use, and disclosure of medical information that is not genetic information about a manifested disease, disorder, or pathological condition is subject to applicable limitations under sections 103(d)(1)- (4) of the

Americans with Disabilities Act (42 U.S.C. 12112(d)(1)-(4)), and regulations at 29 CFR 1630.13, 1630.14, and 1630.16."[85] In its discussion of the final regulations, the EEOC notes that one commenter had expressed concern that individuals who have a manifested genetic disease that is not yet substantially limiting may not be covered under either law. The EEOC declined to address this issue, stating that it had no authority to expand the coverage of GINA. However, the EEOC observed that with the enactment of the ADA Amendments Act (ADAAA),[86] which expanded the definition of disability under the ADA, it is less likely that there would be a significant number of individuals who would not be covered by either act.[87]

Both the EEOC rules and the HHS interim final rules add a definition for the terms "manifestation" and "manifested." Specifically, the rules define these terms to mean a disease, disorder, or pathological condition that has been or could "reasonably be diagnosed by a health care professional with appropriate training and expertise in the field of medicine involved." The rules add further that a "disease, disorder, or pathological condition is not manifested if a diagnosis is based principally on genetic information."[88]

The addition of these definitions may address the concern noted by the commenter (above) regarding those individuals with a manifested genetic disease that is not yet substantially limiting. The definitions have the effect of expanding the applicability of the protections under both titles by further delimiting their exception through the exclusion of individuals with a manifested disease diagnosed principally on genetic information. This implies that the diagnosis was not carried out in the context of, or made based on, the existence of signs or symptoms of the disease or disorder, and appears likely to include those individuals with a manifested (i.e., diagnosed) genetic disease that is not yet substantially limiting (i.e., no substantial signs or symptoms).

Authorization of Appropriations and Effective Date

Such sums as may be necessary are authorized to be appropriated. The effective date of GINA is eighteen months after the date of enactment.

Title III—Miscellaneous Provisions

GINA includes a severability provision. If any provision of the act is declared unconstitutional, the remainder of the act is not to be affected.

Section 16(e) of the Fair Labor Standards Act[89] regarding child labor protections is amended.

Issues for Consideration

The enactment of GINA raises some issues for consideration. Educating the public and health care providers about the scope and application of GINA will be an important part of the implementation phase. Recent data indicate that awareness of the law amongst the public is limited. A 2008 survey reported that, "only 16 percent of respondents to the survey knew that there were laws that protect the privacy of genetic information, and only one-quarter of those felt that protections were sufficient."[90] A similar survey conducted in 2010 found that awareness of laws protecting privacy held steady at 16%, with 77% of Americans unsure whether they are protected by law.[91] Educational efforts are particularly relevant because there are several limitations to the scope of the law of which the public and practitioners should be made aware in order to avoid confusion or misunderstanding.

Importantly, the scope of the law is limited to the settings of health insurance and employment. It does not cover the following: long term care insurance; life insurance; short-term disability insurance; or long-term disability insurance. Moving forward, this distinction may need to be presented clearly to the public, so there is not an expectation of blanket protection from genetic discrimination in all settings where genetic information may be disclosed, requested, required or used. The HHS proposed rule implementing §105 ("Privacy and confidentiality") of Title I may extend certain of GINA's protections to encompass long term care insurance; this is still to be determined pending publication of the final rule. If this interpretation were to be maintained in the final rule, it would be limited to the use of genetic information for underwriting purposes, as required by §105, and would not act to extend the protections established in Sections 101-104 of Title I to long term care insurance.

In addition, GINA does not necessarily extend protections against discrimination in health insurance and employment to individuals with manifested diseases or disorders, genetic or otherwise. Specific provisions in Titles I and II clarify that health insurers and employers will not be in violation of GINA if they utilize specified information about, or knowledge of, a manifested disease or disorder to establish premiums, set enrollment eligibility or preexisting exclusion requirements, or make employment decisions. Again, educational efforts may be useful in ensuring that the public is aware of relevant limitations in the scope of the law.

Finally, the recent passage of the Patient Protection and Affordable Care Act of 2010 (P.L. 111- 148), as amended by the Health Care Education

Reconciliation Act of 2010 (P.L. 111-152), may affect GINA, and Title I provisions in particular. PPACA established a number of reforms to the private health insurance market, limiting insurers' ability in many cases to use health status or factors to discriminate in the issuance or renewal of policies. In addition, provisions in PPACA address employer wellness programs, and the information that such programs may collect from employees. This intersects with GINA in that family history or other genetic information may be requested by the employer in the context of such programs.

End Notes

[1] The Human Genome Project, begun in 1990, was a 13-year effort coordinated and funded by the U.S. Department of Energy and the National Institutes of Health to identify all of the protein-coding genes in human DNA; determine the sequence of the 3 billion chemical bases that make up human DNA; store this information in databases; develop tools for data analysis; and address the ethical, legal, and social issues (ELSI) that may arise from the project. For more detailed information see "The National Human Genome Research Institute," http://www.genome.gov/, and "Human Genome Project Information," http://www.ornl.gov/sci/techresources/Human_Genome/home.shtml.

[2] "International Human Genome Sequencing Consortium Describes Finished Human Genome Sequence," Oct., 20, 2004, at http://www.genome.gov/12513430.

[3] For a discussion of the Equal Employment Opportunity Commission (EEOC) regulations for Title II of GINA see CRS Report R41527, *The Genetic Information Nondiscrimination Act (GINA): Final Employment Regulations*, by Nancy Lee Jones.

[4] Dr. Collins stepped down as Director of the National Human Genome Research Institute to assume the position of Director of the National Institutes of Health. For more information on NHGRI, please see http://www.genome.gov/.

[5] Testimony of Francis S. Collins, former Director, National Human Genome Research Institute, National Institutes of Health, Before the Subcommittee on Health of the House Committee on Energy and Commerce (May 22, 2003).

[6] For more information on the status of genetic tests and further discussion of what constitutes "genetic information," see CRS Report RL33832, *Genetic Testing: Scientific Background for Policymakers*, by Amanda K. Sarata.

[7] The group working on these issues is referred to as the Ethical, Legal and Social Implications (ELSI) program. See http://www.genome.gov/page.cfm?pageID=10001618.

[8] Testimony by Dr. Francis Collins, former Director, National Center for Human Genome Research, before the Senate Committee on Labor and Human Resources (Mar. 6, 1996). See also, Hudson, Rothenberg, Andrews, Kahn, and Collins, "Genetic Discrimination and Health Insurance: An Urgent Need for Reform," 270 *Science* 391 (Oct. 20, 1995); Annas, Glantz, and Roche, "Drafting the Genetic Privacy Act: Science, Policy and Practical Considerations," 23 *J. of Law, Medicine and Ethics* 360 (1995); Gostin, "Genetic Discrimination: The Use of Genetically Based Diagnostic and Prognostic Tests by Employers and Insurers," 17 *Am. J. of Law & Med.* 109 (1991); Rothstein, Mark, *Genetic Secrets: Protecting Privacy and Confidentiality in the Genetic Era* (1997).

[9] Testimony of Francis S. Collins, former Director, National Human Genome Research Institute, National Institutes of Health, before the Senate Health, Education, Labor and Pensions Committee (July 20, 2000).

[10] But see *Norman-Bloodsaw v. Lawrence Berkeley Laboratory,* 135 F.3d 1260 (9th Cir. 1998), where blood tests for sickle cell trait were found to give rise to a Title VII claim. See also the discussion of the Americans with Disabilities Act, *supra*, and Geller, Alper, Billings, Barash, Beckwith, and Natowicz, "Individual, Family, and Societal Dimensions of Genetic Discrimination: A Case Study Analysis," 2 *Science and Engineering Ethics* 71 (1996), which found that a number of institutions, including health and life insurance companies, health care providers, blood banks, adoption agencies, the military, and schools, were reported to have engaged in genetic discrimination against asymptomatic individuals. This study has been criticized by the insurance industry as relying on anecdotal information. See American Council of Life Insurance, "Statement Regarding the Council for Responsible Genetics 'Study' on Genetic Discrimination" (Apr. 11, 1996).

[11] Meeting of the Secretary's Advisory Committee on Genetics, Health, and Society, October 2005. Accessed at http://oba.od.nih.gov/oba/SACGHS/meetings/October2005/White.pdf on May 31, 2011.

[12] Cogent Research, "Americans' Concern about the Privacy of Their Genetic Information Reaches New High," Accessed at http://www.cogentresearch.com/news/Press%20Releases/CGAT%202010_press%20release%20-%20Privacy%20Concerns%20-%2001-10-11.pdf on May 26, 2011.

[13] Highlights and transcripts of Jan. 27, 2000, testimony can be found on the SACGT website at http://oba.od.nih.gov/oba/sacgt/reports/Public%20Consultation%20Summary.pdf. Transcripts of the Oct. 18, 2004, testimony can be found on the SACGHS website at http://oba.od.nih.gov/SACGHS/sacghs_past_meeting_2004_oct_18.html.

[14] From a letter from SACGT to Secretary Tommy Thompson, May 3, 2001, at http://oba.od.nih.gov/oba/sacgt/ltr_to_secDHHS5-3-01.pdf.

[15] Department of Labor, Department of Health and Human Services, Equal Employment Opportunity Commission, Department of Justice, "Genetic Information and the Workplace," Jan. 20, 1998, http://www.dol.gov/oasam/programs/history/herman/reports/genetics.htm.

[16] National Council on Disability, "Position Paper on Genetic Discrimination Legislation," at http://www.ncd.gov/publications/2002/March42002.

[17] 42 U.S.C. §12101 et seq. For a detailed discussion of the ADA see CRS Report 98-921, *The Americans with Disabilities Act (ADA): Statutory Language and Recent Issues*, by Nancy Lee Jones.

[18] 42 U.S.C. §12102, as amended by P.L. 110-325. §4(a). For a more detailed discussion of the ADA Amendments Act see CRS Report RL34691, *The ADA Amendments Act: P.L. 110-325*, by Nancy Lee Jones.

[19] Rep. Owens stated that "[t]hese protections of the ADA will also benefit individuals who are identified through genetic tests as being carriers of a disease-associated gene. There is a record of genetic discrimination against such individuals, most recently during sickle cell screening programs in the 1970s. With the advent of new forms of genetic testing, it is even more critical that the protections of the ADA be in place." 136 Cong. Rec. H 4623 (daily ed. July 12, 1990) (remarks of Rep. Owens). Similarly, Rep. Edwards and Rep. Waxman also stated that individuals who are carriers of a disease-associated gene may not be discriminated against under the ADA. 136 Cong. Rec. H 4625 (daily ed. July 12, 1990) (Statement of Rep. Edwards); *Id.* at H 4627 (Statement of Rep. Waxman).

[20] The EEOC alleged that Burlington Northern Sante Fe (BNSF) Railroad tested its employees for a genetic marker linked to carpal tunnel syndrome in an attempt to address a high number of repetitive stress injuries leading to employee compensation. The EEOC and BNSF reached a settlement agreement rejecting the testing of employees for the genetic marker. See Paul Miller, EEOC commissioner, "Analyzing Genetic Discrimination in the Workplace," 12 Human Genome News (Feb. 2002) at http://www.ornl.gov/sci/techresources/Human_Genome/publicat/hgn/v12n1/09workplace.shtml.

[21] Testimony of Janiori Goldman before the House Committee on Energy and Commerce, Subcommittee on Health, 107th Cong., 1st sess. (Mar. 22, 2001).

[22] Equal Employment Opportunity Commission, Compliance Manual, vol. 2, section 902, order 915.002,902-45 (1995). It is also possible that Title VII of the Civil Rights Act of 1964, 42 U.S.C. § 2000e et seq., may provide some protection against certain kinds of genetic discrimination since an argument could be made that discrimination based on genetic disorders that are more common in certain racial or ethnic groups, such as sickle cell disease, is prohibited under Title VII. There are relatively few genetic conditions that have a strong connection with a racial or ethnic group, thus limiting the scope of potential coverage. However, in *Norman-Bloodsaw v. Lawrence Berkeley Laboratory,* 135 F.3d 1260 (9th Cir. 1998), blood tests for sickle cell trait were found to give rise to a Title VII claim.

[23] 42 U.S.C. §12102(2).

[24] See *Sutton v. United Airlines*, 527 U.S. 471 (1999); *Murphy v. United Parcel Service, Inc.*,527 U.S. 516 (1999).

[25] Statement of Commissioner Paul Steven Miller, U.S. Equal Employment Opportunity Commission, before the Senate Committee on Health, Education, Labor and Pensions, July 20, 2000.

[26] For a discussion of the Supreme Court's ADA decisions see CRS Report RL31401, *The Americans with Disabilities Act: Supreme Court Decisions*, by Nancy Lee Jones.

[27] http://www.eeoc.gov/policy/docs/guidance-genetic.html

[28] 75 FED. REG. 68929 (November 9, 2010).

[29] National Conference of State Legislatures, Genetics Tables, State Genetics Employment Laws, http://www.ncsl.org/programs/health/genetics/ndiscrim.htm.

[30] *Id.*

[31] National Conference of State Legislatures Genetics Tables, State Genetic Nondiscrimination in Health Insurance, http://www.ncsl.org/programs/health/genetics/ndishlth.htm.

[32] National Conference of State Legislatures Genetics Tables, State Genetic Privacy Laws, http://www.ncsl.org/programs/health/genetics/prt.htm.

[33] *Id.*

[34] 29 U.S.C. §§1001-1145.

[35] Kaiser Family Foundation, "Employer Health Benefits, Annual Survey 2007," accessed at http://www.kff.org/insurance/7672/upload/76723.pdf.

[36] 149 Cong. Rec. S12394-12508 (daily ed. Oct. 4, 2003).

[37] "Genetic Non-Discrimination: Examining the Implications for Workers and Employers" Subcommittee on Employer-Employee Relations, House Committee on Education and Workforce (July 22, 2004).

[38] 42 U.S.C. §2000ff(4).

[39] 74 Fed. Reg. 51644 (October 7, 2009).

[40] 74 Fed. Reg. 51698 (October 7, 2009).

[41] 74 Fed. Reg. 18808 (April 24, 2010).

[42] 75 Fed. Reg. 68916 (November 9, 2010).

[43] 42 U.S.C. §2000ff(7).
[44] 42 U.S.C. §2000ff-9.
[45] 29 C.F.R. §1635.3(f)(2); 75 Fed. Reg. 68933 (November 9, 2010).
[46] 29 C.F.R. §1635.3(f)(3); 75 Fed. Reg. 68933 (November 9, 2010).
[47] 74 Fed. Reg. 51665 (October 7, 2009).
[48] 74 Fed. Reg. 51668 (October 7, 2009).
[49] 74 Fed. Reg. 51679 (October 7, 2009).
[50] 74 Fed. Reg. 51680 (October 7, 2009).
[51] 74 Fed. Reg. 51687 (October 7, 2009).
[52] 45 C.F.R. Part 46.
[53] 74 Fed. Reg. 51709.
[54] 74 Fed. Reg. 51703, 51709.
[55] 74 Fed. Reg. 51665 (October 7, 2009).
[56] 75 Fed. Reg. 68912 (November 9, 2010). For a discussion of these regulation see CRS Report R41527, *The Genetic Information Nondiscrimination Act (GINA): Final Employment Regulations*, by Nancy Lee Jones.
[57] 42 U.S.C. §§2000e(f)(employees), 2000e(b)(employers).
[58] 42 U.S.C. §2000e-16c(a).
[59] 2 U.S.C. §1301.
[60] 29 C.F.R. §1635.2(c); 75 FED. REG. 68932 (November 9, 2010). The Supreme Court in Robinson v. Shell Oil Co., 519 U.S. 337, 346 (1997), held that the term employee under Title VII, which is referenced in the definition in GINA, includes former employees.
[61] In its regulations, the EEOC, instead of referencing the different categories of employers covered by GINA, refers to them as "covered entities." 29 C.F.R. §1635.2(b); 75 FED. REG. 68932 (Nov. 9, 2010).
[62] 42 U.S.C. §2000ff-1(a)-(b)(employers); 42 U.S.C. §2000ff-2(a)-(b)(employment agencies); 42 U.S.C. §2000ff-3(a)-(b)(labor organizations); 42 U.S.C. §2000ff-4(a)(b)(training programs).
[63] 42 U.S.C. §2000ff-1(b)(employers); 42 U.S.C. §2000ff-2(b)(employment agencies); 42 U.S.C. §2000ff-3(b)(labor organizations); 42 U.S.C. §2000ff-4(b)(training programs).
[64] 42 U.S.C. §2000ff-1(c)(employers); 42 U.S.C. §2000ff-2(c)(employment agencies); 42 U.S.C. §2000ff-3(c)(labor organizations); 42 U.S.C. §2000ff-4(c)(training programs).
[65] H.Rept. 110-28, Part 1 at 37 (March 5, 2007).
[66] 29 C.F.R. § 1635.3(b); 75 FED. REG. 68933 (November 9, 2010).
[67] For a discussion of the legal issues involving wellness programs generally, see CRS Report R40661, *Wellness Programs: Selected Legal Issues*, coordinated by Nancy Lee Jones.
[68] 29 C.F.R. §1635.8(b)(2), 75 FED. REG. 68935 (November 9, 2010).
[69] 29 C.F.R. §1635.8(b)(2)(ii)(A), 75 FED. REG. 68935 (November 9, 2010).
[70] 29 C.F.R. §1635.8(b)(2)(ii)(B), 75 FED. REG. 68935 (November 9, 2010).
[71] H.Rept. 110-28, Part 1 at 38 (March 5, 2007).
[72] 29 C.F.R. §1635.8(b)(3), 75 FED. REG. 68936 (November 9, 2010).
[73] *Id.*
[74] 29 C.F.R. §1635.8(b)(4), 75 FED. REG. 68936 (November 9, 2010).
[75] 75 Fed. Reg. 68925 (November 9, 2010).
[76] *Id.*
[77] 75 Fed. Reg. 68926 (November 9, 2010).
[78] 42 U.S.C. §12112(d)(3)(B).
[79] 29 C.F.R. §1635.9, 75 FED. REG. 68937 (November 9, 2010).
[80] 75 Fed. Reg. 68927 (November 9, 2010).

[81] 42 U.S.C. §2000e-4 et seq

[82] 29 C.F.R. §1635.10(b), 75 Fed. Reg. 68938 (November 9, 2010).

[83] 42 U.S.C. §2000e-2(k).

[84] 154 Cong. Rec. H2972 (daily ed. May 1, 2008)(statement of Rep. Dingell).

[85] 29 C.F.R. §1635.12, 75 Fed. Reg. 68939 (November 9, 2010).

[86] P.L. 110-325. For a discussion of the ADAAA see CRS Report RL34691, *The ADA Amendments Act: P.L. 110-325*, by Nancy Lee Jones.

[87] 75 Fed. Reg. 68931 (November 9, 2010).

[88] 74 Fed. Reg. 51666 (October 7, 2009) and 75 Fed. Reg. 68917 (November 9, 2010).

[89] 29 U.S.C. §216(e).

[90] SACGHS, "Genetics Education and Training of Health Care Professionals, Public Health Providers, and Consumers," (May 2010) accessed at http://oba.od.nih.gov/oba/SACGHS/SACGHS%20Draft%20Genetics%20Education%20and%20Training%20Report.pdf#page=56 on July 1, 2010.

[91] Council for Responsible Genetics, "Genetic Privacy Worries on the Rise," accessed at http://www.councilforresponsiblegenetics.org/genewatch/GeneWatchPage.aspx?pageId=324 on May 26, 2011.

In: Genetic Information, Health Laws ... ISBN: 978-1-61942-176-9
Editors: Gossling and Richards

Chapter 6

GENETIC EXCEPTIONALISM: GENETIC INFORMATION AND PUBLIC POLICY*

Amanda K. Sarata

SUMMARY

The Human Genome Project, from inception through completion, has generated a great deal of debate over the appropriate uses, as well as potential misuses, of genetic information. Legislation that is specific to genetics is predicated on the concept of genetic exceptionalism, or the premise that genetic information is unique and, therefore, merits both special and different, or exceptional, treatment. As applied to public policy, this translates into genetics-specific legislative approaches to various health policy issues, such as the oversight of genetic tests, privacy, and discrimination in health insurance. Amidst great concern over the potential for the misuse of genetic information, most states passed genetics legislation during the past decade and a half in areas such as genetic privacy, genetic discrimination in health insurance, and genetic discrimination in employment. A genetic exceptionalist approach was taken by lawmakers in the Genetic Information Nondiscrimination Act of 2008 (P.L. 110-233).

This report provides an overview of the nature of genetic information and its implications for individuals, family, and society. Individuals

* This is an edited, reformatted and augmented version of a Congressional Research Service publication, CRS Report for Congress RL34376, from www.crs.gov, dated on March 19, 2010.

utilize genetic information to guide health care and other decisions, when possible, and may experience anxiety as a result of genetic test results. Genetic test results for an individual may often be informative for other close family members and thus influence their care decisions. Society must grapple with the effect genetic information may have on our conception of disease, as well as its impact on issues like privacy and equity. The report ends by summarizing the main issues involved with a genetic exceptionalist approach to public policy, including defining genetic information; physically separating genetic information from other medical information; unintended disparities between "genetic" and "nongenetic" disease; and the effect of legislation on participation in genetic research, on uptake of genetic technology and on the delivery of high quality health care.

INTRODUCTION

Advances in human genetics, and especially the completion of the Human Genome Project, have focused attention on the potentially numerous ways that genetic information may be used to improve and benefit health and health care. Despite excitement about the anticipated benefits that the use of such information may generate, lawmakers have raised concern about the potential for misuse of this information as well. Genetic information can be defined in many ways, but for the purposes of this report, it means information about genes, gene products, or inherited characteristics generated through either genetic testing or analysis of family history.

The term "genetic exceptionalism" refers to the concept that genetic information is inherently unique, should receive special consideration, and should be treated differently in law. This idea is based on the supposition that genetic information itself embodies several characteristics that may make it special and differentiate it from other medical or even personal information. According to the perspective of genetic exceptionalism, the characteristics of genetic information that make it different include the following: it can be predictive of future disease; it is a unique identifier; it can reveal information about family members; it is vertically transmitted (passed from parent to child); it can impact communities; it can be used to discriminate and stigmatize; and it can cause serious psychological harm. In addition, although not specific to genetic information, the following characteristics also describe genetic information: it can be obtained from small samples (possibly without consent); it may be used for purposes other than those for which it was collected; it is of interest to third parties (such as employers and insurers); it may be important for determining susceptibility to disease and effectiveness of treatment; and it can be recovered from stored specimens after many years.[1] These characteristics are not unique to genetic information; other medical information may also have some of these characteristics in common with genetic information. However, it may be argued that there is little medical or personal information that shares *all* of these characteristics with genetic information.

Genetic information is viewed as powerful, perhaps uniquely so, by society and has been regarded with some degree of awe and respect not afforded other types of health or personal information.[2] This may be due to the sense that genetic information is immutable and, therefore, that its use merits more caution than might the use of other information. This heightened caution may be warranted simply because of the perception that genetic information cannot be modified or altered, and that it is not chosen by the individual who bears it. The differential regard for genetic information may also be related to the idea of genetic determinism, or the concept that our genes exclusively predict or foretell our fate, including health, behavior, and physical characteristics. Although efforts have been made by responsible scientists to disabuse the public of this notion by stressing the role of environmental factors in disease, it is still fairly persistent, as seen in overly glowing portrayals of genetic discoveries and technologies by the media. It is difficult to specifically determine what gave rise to the concept of genetic exceptionalism; however, it does appear that, broadly, the public regards genetic information as particularly sensitive and perhaps even as unique.

The influence of the concept of genetic exceptionalism is reflected in genetics-specific public policy at the state level, proposed legislation at the federal level, and existing federal law. At the federal level, Congress passed the Genetic Information Nondiscrimination Act of 2008 (GINA, P.L. 110-233), which employs an exceptionalist approach. A number of states have passed genetic nondiscrimination legislation that places various restrictions on health insurers' use, collection, or acquisition of genetic information to restrict or deny health insurance coverage. Similarly, a majority of states have passed legislation to protect the privacy of genetic information or to prohibit employers from using such information to discriminate against employees. Because the idea of genetic exceptionalism has had a significant influence on public policy to date, Congress may want to consider how to treat genetic information in future legislative efforts, for example, in the areas of personalized medicine or oversight of laboratory testing.

This report provides an overview of the implications of genetic information for individuals, family, and society; examines public opinion about genetic information; and summarizes the main policy arguments for and against incorporating genetic exceptionalism into public policy.

GENETIC INFORMATION VS. OTHER MEDICAL INFORMATION

The differences between genetic information and other types of medical information have important implications for the individual, for families, and for society as a whole.[3] The discussion below provides a broad overview of these implications, but recognizes that there may be specific examples of nongenetic tests that have the same implications as genetic tests. However, the discussion below is meant to provide a general comparison across the two categories of tests— genetic versus nongenetic—and the information they generate.

Implications for Individuals

Genetic tests are similar to many other medical tests in that they are often used to diagnose a disease or condition. Most of these diagnostic tests, both genetic and nongenetic, provide information about treatable maladies. Unlike most other medical tests, however, genetic tests may be used to determine that a currently healthy individual is susceptible to—at increased risk of developing—a particular illness or condition (susceptibility genetic testing). Genetic tests may also be used to predict that a currently healthy person will develop an illness or condition in the future with certainty (predictive genetic testing). It is often the case that many of the illnesses and conditions tested for using predictive or susceptibility testing cannot be cured or prevented by any currently available medical intervention. For example, a genetic test is available for Huntington's disease, a disease for which no prevention or cure (or even effective treatment) currently exists.

Because of this general lack of curative measures, sometimes the only options for reducing one's risk of future disease rely on modification of personal health related behaviors; for example, undergoing frequent screening, eating healthy foods, and exercising regularly. It is unclear how knowledge of genetic risk factors will influence the modification of such behaviors. While some individuals may modify their behavior because of knowledge of their genetic risk factors, some may have the perception that because they cannot change their genetic makeup, modifying their behavior will have little effect on decreasing their risk for disease. It is possible that these individuals may even increase unhealthy behaviors out of a sense of hopelessness. If no preventive or curative options exist, predictive genetic test results may increase a patient's anxiety level if they are positive or provide a false sense of reassurance if they are negative. Susceptibility genetic test results may also increase anxiety if they indicate an increased risk of disease while offering no options for mitigating this risk. For example, a certain allele, the APOE4 allele, has been found to increase an individual's risk of developing Alzheimer's disease. However, testing for this particular allele has been discouraged by health professionals because Alzheimer's disease cannot be prevented or cured, and, therefore, knowing one's risk status may simply increase anxiety. Furthermore, the actual increase in risk is not absolute in any sense; one may carry two copies of the APOE4 allele and still not develop Alzheimer's disease, while one may carry no copies of the APOE4 allele and still develop the disease.

Unlike most other medical testing, genetic testing may unintentionally reveal information about an individual or may reveal information with unknown significance given current scientific knowledge. For example, genetic testing may reveal unanticipated instances of non-paternity (where it is revealed that the purported father is in fact not the father). The development of microarray technology provides an increasingly cost-effective mechanism for testing hundreds or even thousands of genetic health indicators at one time.[4] Genetic testing on this scale could likely lead not only to the revelation of an enormous amount of health information about individuals, but also to a large amount of unexpected health information. This raises concerns about informed consent, as obtaining truly voluntary informed consent for each individual test might be prohibitively time consuming. Banking and storage of this vast amount of information, along with personal identifiers, provides unique challenges to existing privacy protections. Consumer advocates caution that although economic incentives favor testing for a large number of genetic characteristics at one time, testing should be limited to allow for thorough informed consent before and genetic counseling both prior to and after testing.

Genetic information can be used not only in the clinical setting, but also by forensic experts and the criminal justice system to identify individuals with a high degree of certainty. Genetic information has been used to help convict and exonerate individuals accused of committing crimes. It has been used to help identify the remains of war and accident victims. Because of these potential applications, tissue samples and certain types of genetic information collected for health care purposes may later be used in law enforcement, and vice versa. The fact that genetic information collected for health care may have forensic applications may increase lawmakers' concern with the increasingly widespread availability and use of genetic information. Concern about use of genetic information in nonhealth settings may also decrease uptake of new genetic technologies in health care and decrease participation in genetic research.

Implications for the Family

Genetic tests for *acquired* markers—genetic changes that an individual does not receive from his or her parents but rather acquires sometime post-conception—have direct medical implications only for the individuals taking the tests.[5] Most other medical tests also have direct medical implications only for the individual taking the test. However, unlike most other medical tests, genetic tests for *inherited* markers—markers that are transmitted from parents to their offspring— have implications for biological relatives of the individual. Parents, siblings, and children have a predictable risk of sharing certain inherited genetic markers. Furthermore, the generally unchanging nature of inherited DNA means that genetic testing for inherited markers can be performed at any stage of human development on most tissue types. This offers the possibility of testing before implantation or prenatally, and may possibly allow for fetal intervention.

Some genetic tests cannot be interpreted for an individual unless other members of her family are also tested. For example, breast cancer genetic testing on the BRCA1 and BRCA2 genes relies on sequencing the entire gene in an affected individual to pinpoint the specific familial mutation. Then other family members may be tested for that specific mutation to help accurately determine if they are at increased risk of developing breast and/or ovarian cancer and, if so, the magnitude of that risk. In those cases, all family members may or may not want to know their test results. Sometimes testing family members can also provide unwelcome information about sensitive issues such as paternity.

Implications for Society

Unlike most other medical information, genetic information challenges traditional medical perceptions of health and disease, what is normal or abnormal, and raises questions about what constitutes manifested disease. For example, lactose intolerance was long thought to be an abnormal state. Research in different populations elucidated that, in fact, it is the normal state, and the ability to digest lactose was the result of mutations that were under strong selective pressure in areas of the world where domestication of animals led to increased consumption of dairy products. These concepts are becoming increasingly blurred as genetic advances uncover the true range of "normal" and "abnormal" in many human traits.

Many experts predict that genetics may soon provide the opportunity to test large groups of people for disease susceptibilities. However, fear caused by the possibility that a job may be lost or insurance may be cancelled—whether real or perceived—affects individuals' decisions regarding seeking potentially beneficial genetic testing in clinical or research settings. If people decline to participate in genetic research in large numbers, the ability of scientists to gather the data that are necessary to determine the utility or ultimately the value of genetic testing may be compromised. This may delay realization of the potential benefits of genetic advances for the larger population. However, recently enacted genetic nondiscrimination legislation at the federal level may serve to counter this concern, at least to some degree.

Genetic information may be used in order to link a person to a distinct group or heritage. This type of information may have consequences, particularly for individuals who have rights based upon heritage, such as Native Americans. Advocates of these groups are wary of the potential effect that genetic testing and information could have on their current rights and protections. Others argue that definitions of race and heredity are irrelevant or that genetic information will not supplant current nongenetic determinants of ancestry. Finally, because the prevalence of disease-causing genes often varies by ethnicity, there is potential for discrimination against groups of people that share similar genetic information.

The meaning of genetic information evolves with scientific progress, which has special implications both for privacy and for equity. In the privacy arena, a person could grant others access to genetic data that is benign by today's standards. However, with scientific advancements these same data may in time reveal more sensitive information. In the equity arena, those with health conditions for which genetic tests currently exist may suffer discrimination in the near future, while those with similarly debilitating health conditions for which there is no genetic test may escape the same discrimination simply by virtue of the current state of science. Certain initiatives in genetic research, such as large-scale banking of genetic information, could raise both privacy and equity concerns, even though they may also have widespread public health benefit— such as facilitating characterization of genetic markers associated with rare adverse drug events.

Public Opinion about Genetic Information

Although there has been an ongoing academic debate about the concept of genetic exceptionalism, it is perhaps more relevant in terms of public policy to examine how the public views genetic information. Several studies have been undertaken in an attempt to elucidate whether the public views genetic information as inherently different from other information, whether it deserves special protections, and who should have access to it. All of these studies were conducted prior to the passage of GINA, however, and it may be the case that with its passage, attitudes about genetic information may change. Studies examining the effect of GINA on attitudes about genetic information could not be identified, perhaps due to the law's relatively recent passage.

To address the question of whether genetic information merits special protections, a 2007 study examined opinions about genetic information through a series of focus groups with members of a health maintenance organization (n=46). Focus groups conducted with these members found that, broadly, participants did not feel that genetic information is special or inherently different from other medical information. In addition, the participants generally felt that all sensitive medical information, including but not limited to genetic information, should be protected. Sensitive medical information was agreed to be that information that has the potential to be used to discriminate against or stigmatize an individual.[6]

A second study compared the experiences, attitudes, and beliefs of persons with genetic conditions (cystic fibrosis and sickle cell disease) to those with other serious medical conditions (diabetes, HIV, breast cancer, and colon cancer) and to persons at risk for developing a disease (breast or colon cancer) due to strong family history. The authors found that in most instances, patients felt strongly that their health information needed to be protected regardless of whether it was genetic. In fact, respondents indicated that information about non-genetic stigmatizing conditions—such as abortion history, mental health history, drug and alcohol history, HIV status, and sexually transmitted disease—needed special protection. Based on their findings, the authors concluded that separate privacy policies for genetic and non-genetic health information would be unwarranted.[7]

Other studies and public opinion polls suggest that patients and members of the community desire and may benefit from additional protections for their genetic information. A 2003 study of 470 people with a family history of colorectal cancer showed that 39% rated their level of concern about genetic discrimination in health insurance as the most significant reason to forego testing. Those individuals with high levels of concern indicated that they would be significantly less likely to consider meeting with a health care professional to discuss genetic testing, or to undergo testing.[8] A 2007 survey by the Center for Genetics and Public Policy found that 93% of survey respondents thought employers should not have access to their genetic test results, and 93% opposed letting insurance companies have access to results.[9] A 2006 survey conducted by Cogent Research found that 72% of survey respondents believe that laws are needed to protect the privacy of genetic information, and 85% believe that if protections are not established, employers would use genetic information discriminate.[10]

Findings from these selected studies suggest that people view genetic information as particularly sensitive, but not more so than other sensitive medical information such as HIV status. These studies also found that people believe that genetic information needs to be kept private from employers or insurers, and that special protections are required to achieve this goal.

POLICY ISSUES

When considering public policy to legislate the treatment of genetic information, Congress may want to address several key issues, such as defining genetic information; physically separating genetic information from other medical information; unintended disparities between "genetic" and "nongenetic" disease; and the effect of legislation on participation in genetic research, on uptake of genetic technology, and on the delivery of high quality health care. Policy makers may take an exceptionalist approach, meaning they may chose to treat genetic information differently from other medical information. For example, GINA takes this approach. Conversely, policy makers may wish to take a non-exceptionalist approach, meaning they may wish to treat genetic information the same way as they treat other medical information. For example, the HIPAA Privacy Rule treats genetic information in a non-exceptional way. Some of the policy issues Congress may want to consider are outlined below.

Defining Genetic vs. Nongenetic Information

If a genetic exceptionalist approach to public policy at the federal level were to be employed, several policy considerations may be raised. Experts highlight the challenge of effectively defining genetic versus nongenetic information for public policy purposes,[11] pointing out that the difficulty associated with attempting such a definition should "give us pause with regard to treating the results of "genetic tests" differently from other clinical findings in the medical record."[12] All disease is now thought to have a genetic component; hence, the term genetic disease is slowly growing more obsolete. Nearly all medical information might arguably be defined as being in part genetic in nature, creating challenges for making such a distinction.

Separation of Genetic Information from Nongenetic Information

In addition, separating genetic from non-genetic information in medical records may pose a real practical challenge. Requirements regarding the separation of different types of medical information may be so complicated and costly as to actually interfere with the delivery of effective and high-quality care. Requirements of this type could potentially further frustrate attempts by physicians to provide optimal care to their patients, and may impede the sharing of relevant medical information.

Importantly, adoption of electronic medical records may facilitate such a separation (both for purposes of maintaining the information and releasing the information).[13] The Personalized Health Care Work Group of the American Health Information Community (AHIC) released a statement in July of 2008 recommending that, if federal policy were developed that would provide for limited access to sensitive medical information in EHRs (i.e., through data masking), genetic/genomic information should be subject to these limitations.[14] The authors argue that genetic information is characterized by a series of attributes that, while not all unique to genetic information, make genetic information unique because they in aggregate characterize such information. They further maintain that in order to realize the promise of personalized medicine, both access to and use of genetic/genomic information must be controlled to a greater extent than it is for other, less sensitive, medical information. Other commentators argue that genetic exceptionalism is an outdated concept. These experts claim that the rest of the information contained in the medical record is highly identifying; that penetrance of the genotype (i.e., how predictive it is and how strongly it correlates therefore to a certain clinical endpoint) may be more important to policy discussions than the fact that the information was generated by genetic technologies; and that in fact, the more clinically relevant the information, the less desirable is a genetic exceptionalist approach.[15] These experts express concern that a genetic excpetionalist approach might interfere with health care providers' ability to provide the best care to patients.

Disparity Vetween Genetic and Nongenetic Disease

Several experts have voiced concern that genetic exceptionalist laws may result in unintended disparities.[16] For example, they argue that such laws may create a situation where individuals affected by a disease or condition with a *known* genetic basis (i.e., breast cancer in the presence of a BRCA1 mutation) would be protected from discrimination while those with breast cancer with no *known* genetic basis would not be protected.

Considerations Regarding Uptake/Utilization of Genetic Technologies and Participation in Genetic Research

Prior to the passage of GINA, experts often asserted that without genetic-specific legislation in place, individuals would not utilize and, therefore, may lose out on, the clinical and other benefits of new genetic technologies out of concern about misuse of their genetic information. In addition, these experts maintained that without protections in place, genetic research would be stifled.[17] It is possible, however, that genetic exceptionalist laws, GINA included, might reinforce perceptions among the public that genetic information is special, unique, or deterministic. Although many argued that protections are needed to encourage participation in genetic research and the uptake of genetic medical technologies and tests, it is possible that reinforcing the notion that genetic information is uniquely powerful (i.e., has such high potential for misuse that it requires its own special protections) might have the unintended consequence of decreasing participation in genetic research or decreasing utilization of important genetic tests that could guide treatment. This is especially potentially a concern if GINA is perceived by the public to be weak or lacking thoroughness in the protection it offers. The recent passage of GINA may provide an opportunity to assess what effect, if any, taking an exceptionalist approach may have on public opinion regarding genetic information; on uptake/utilization of genetic technologies; and on participation in genetics research.

Conversely, in an environment where special protections were not extended to genetic information, patients might have been hesitant to share relevant genetic information because of concerns about possible misuse, and health care providers might have difficulty providing the best care to their patients.[18] With a non-exceptionalist policy approach, it could have been challenging to adequately safeguard genetic information. A broader law may be more unwieldy and, therefore, could have created challenges to providing the appropriate protections for medical information with varying degrees of sensitivity. As there is some evidence that the public views genetic information as deserving of special protections, if not of being special itself, treating genetic information the same as other medical information may not have resonated with the public (see "Public Opinion about Genetic Information" above).

End Notes

[1] Nuffield Council on Bioethics. Pharmacogenetics: ethical issues. (2003), at http://www.nuffieldbioethics.org/fileLibrary/pdf/pharmacogenetics_report.pdf.

[2] Roche PA and GJ Annas, "Protecting genetic privacy," Nature Reviews Genetics, 2:392-396, 2001.

[3] For more information about genetic testing, see CRS Report RL33832, *Genetic Testing: Scientific Background for Policymakers*, by Amanda K. Sarata.

[4] Microarray technology is defined as "a new way of studying how large numbers of genes interact with each other and how a cell's regulatory networks control vast batteries of genes simultaneously." Accessed at http://www.genome.gov/glossary.cfm?key= microarray%20technology.

[5] For example, the onco*type* Dx test offered by Genomic Health profiles a tumor's gene expression patterns to determine whether the tumor is likely to spread or respond to different types of treatment. Expression patterns in tumors are largely due to acquired mutations.

[6] Diergaarde B. et al., "Genetic Information: Special or Not? Responses From Focus Groups With Members of a Health Maintenance Organization," *American Journal of Genetics Part A*, 143A: 564-569, 2007.

[7] Plantinga L. et al., "Disclosure, Confidentiality, and Families: Experiences and Attitudes of Those with Genetic Versus Nongenetic Medical Conditions," *American Journal of Medicine*, General Part C, vol. 119C (2003), pp. 51-59.

[8] Hadley D.W. et al., "Genetic counseling and testing in families with hereditary nonpolyposis colorectal cancer," *Arch Intern Med*, 163(5): 573-82, 2003.

[9] Williams S., "The Impact of Genetic Discrimination," *Genetics and Public Policy Center Issue Brief*, Updated April 2007.

[10] Presentation by Ms. Christy White at the Ninth Meeting of the Secretary's Advisory Committee on Genetics, Health, and Society. March 28, 2006. Accessed at http://oba.od.nih.gov/oba/SACGHS/meetings/March2006/white.pdf.

[11] Rothstein, M.A., "Genetic Exceptionalism and Legislative Pragmatism," *The Journal of Law, Medicine, and Ethics*, 35(2):59-65, 2007.

[12] Burke, W and JP Evans. (2008) "Genetic exceptionalism. Too much of a good thing?" *Genetics in Medicine* 10(7): 500-501.

[13] Ibid.

[14] McGuire AL et. al. (2008) "Confidentiality, privacy and security of genetic and genomic test information in electronic health records: points to consider." *Genetics in Medicine* 10(7): 495-499.

[15] Burke, W and JP Evans. (2008) "Genetic exceptionalism. Too much of a good thing?" *Genetics in Medicine* 10(7): 500-501.

[16] Diergaarde B. et al., "Genetic Information: Special or Not? Responses From Focus Groups With Members of a Health Maintenance Organization," *Am J Genet Part A*, 143A: 564-569, 2007.

[17] Slaughter L.M., "Your Genes and Privacy," *Science*, 316(5826): 797, 2007.

[18] Hadley D.W. et al., "Genetic counseling and testing in families with hereditary nonpolyposis colorectal cancer," *Arch Intern Med*, 163(5): 573-82, 2003.

Chapter Sources

Chapter 1 - This is an edited, reformatted and augmented version of a Congressional Research Service publication, R41314, dated December 13, 2010.

Chapter 2 - This is an edited, reformatted and augmented version of a Congressional Research Service publication, R40791, dated February 16, 2010.

Chapter 3 - This is an edited, reformatted and augmented version of a Congressional Research Service publication, R40661, dated December 13, 2010.

Chapter 4 – This is an edited, reformatted and augmented version of a Congressional Research Service publication, R41527, dated December 9, 2010

Chapter 5 - This is an edited, reformatted and augmented version of a Congressional Research Service publication, RL34584, dated June 13, 2011.

Chapter 6 – This is an edited, reformatted and augmented version of a Congressional Research Service publication, RL34376, dated March 19, 2010.

INDEX

A

B

C

D

E

F

T

U

V

W